TEN STEPS

TO

YOUR

BEST LIFE

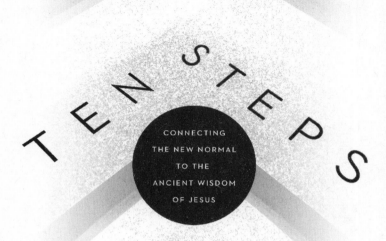

TEN STEPS

CONNECTING
THE NEW NORMAL
TO THE
ANCIENT WISDOM
OF JESUS

TO

YOUR

BEST LIFE

BRENT CROWE

B&H
PUBLISHING
NASHVILLE, TENNESSEE

For Gabe, Charis, Za'Riah, Mercy, Zi'Yon, and Ary-girl

You are everyday proof that Jesus is able "to do above and beyond all that we ask or think."

Being your dad is the beautiful joy of my life.

Acknowledgments

I wish to begin by thanking the love of my life, Christina. Your very embrace is my home in this world. Thank you for preaching sermons no one will ever hear but that keep me believing *with God all things are possible*. To my amazing team at Student Leadership University, I am so grateful to labor beside you in the mission to help a generation think, dream, and lead at the feet of Jesus. To Anna, my brilliant assistant, thanks for walking through this process, always being willing to do whatever it took to help.

To the students we serve through the SLU Journey. You are the reason I get out of bed and go to work every day. I believe you will change the world by answering the question: "What would I do for the glory of God if I knew I would not fail?" Keep dreaming, keep believing, keep exploring . . . knowing that if your dream is of God, he will bring it to fruition.

To my parents, thank you in advance for buying a box of books. You are relentless in your support and I am forever grateful. To the mentors and friends who took my calls and helped me wrestle ideas to the ground, your wise counsel is often the catalyst I needed to be creative. To the pastors, youth pastors, and various ministry leaders that trust me to preach and teach the Bible at your churches, schools, and events, thank you for trusting me.

Finally, and of course most importantly, thank you Jesus for walking onto the playground of my life and choosing me first. Thank you for choosing me simply because you loved me before I could ever love you in return.

Contents

Introduction

Blue Tarps

I live in central Florida. We are no stranger to hurricanes and storms. I remember one particular hurricane season some years back when we experienced four very significant storms in just a six-week period. Living in the state's center provides us protection from the full force of storms that coastal cities experience. But it also means that if a storm hits anywhere near us, we experience the outer bands of winds, flash flooding, and all the destruction left in their wake.

After the first storm, which caused some roof damage and temporary power outages, people cleaned up their yards by cutting up fallen trees and limbs and putting them on the curbs in front of their houses. Then, another storm hit, turning logs and limbs into projectiles that wreaked havoc on whatever structure stood in its way. Fast-forward two more storms and a month or so, and Orlando and the surrounding cities were hurting. In my neighborhood, there were more roofs with blue tarps than intact roofs.

For at least the next year, every time I flew home, I knew I was getting close when I would start observing the sea of blue tarps as far as the eye could see. A blue tarp is essentially a

Band-Aid on your roof to keep it from leaking until someone can repair it. It was rather sad to look out at the sea of Band-Aids week after week, month after month.

The pandemic of 2020–21 felt like waves of one storm after another pounding against the shores of our souls. And with each storm, stuff got stirred up and thrown around, hurting whoever was in its path. By "stuff," I mean all the painful realities of enduring a once-every-hundred-years event that turns lives upside down and shakes us relentlessly. It was a season that took immeasurably more than it gave.

At first, it seemed as if the pandemic stripped society down to only the bare essentials for living. Theme parks, concerts, sporting events, and even graduation ceremonies were canceled. But then, it started impacting people we knew. The virus was "out there" in the world, and we began to realize that we might have to come in contact with someone who tested positive. Contact tracing, masking up, and social distancing became part of the rhythm of living. Hospitals were at capacity, and ICU beds became the rarest of commodities. Some hospitals even converted their parking garages into a sanitized and patchwork field infirmary. Frontline workers were, and still are, the brave and unyielding unsung heroes who didn't have the word *quit* in their vocabulary.

The longer the pandemic continued, the more we realized our silver linings were made of tinfoil. People consumed exponentially more alcohol, with liquor sales skyrocketing. Domestic violence increased, as well as a myriad of other abuses. There was a profound impact on the mental health of many in the storm. By June 2020, just a few months after we had even learned the word *COVID-19*, the Centers for Disease Control and Prevention reported 40 percent of adults were struggling with mental health and an increase in substance use.[1] All in all, there was an increase in anxiety, depression, substance abuse, and suicidal thoughts. It was an unprecedented time that caused medical, social, and economic mayhem across the globe.

And as the vaccine emerged on the scene, there was a feeling that the pandemic would come to an end. The sunlight began to break through the storm-filled clouds. We hoped for finality. The chapter needed to end, the page needed to turn, and the story needed to move in a more hopeful direction.

But, as with all storms, when the sun shines, the cleanup had only just begun and took some time.

We were a sea of Band-Aids. The storm had subsided, but blue tarps were everywhere to be found. Since the pandemonium of the pandemic had dissipated, there was a desire to recapture what was once lost. Like a gravitational pull for moons orbiting a planet, our souls seemed to draw to the excess and comfort of days gone by. It is human nature to imagine the good old days to be better than they actually were and remember the bad days as darker. As a species, we are prone to exaggeration. The challenge, however, isn't to regain a mythical and fantastical version of the past. Instead, it is to reimagine an abundant vision for the future.

I've written this book for anyone who doesn't want to live under a blue tarp anymore.[2]

Your Best Life Defined

I know this will sound naive or crazy, but there is a life to be discovered in the ashes of the pandemic, and it's better than we could have ever imagined. If you were to be honest, there is something in your soul that is longing for it. Guess what? Rising from the ashes to a glorious possibility is something that God wants for you. In fact, he specializes in it!

This isn't a book filled with fancy words intended to impress; it is a sacred and straightforward strategy meant to move past the blue-tarp phase of life and discover something new. Truth be told, I think God sometimes looks on and chuckles at our lofty attempts at expressing our spirituality. Much like a parent watching a child recite a speech with big words, he smiles and is patient as we clumsily reach for the top-shelf ideas.

We are like a high school drama club performing Shakespeare with little acting skills and a shoestring budget for production, but God is in the front row beaming with pride as we do our best to remember and deliver the lines with gumption. Let us never forget that God is fatherly. This is why "God sent the Spirit of his Son into our hearts, crying, '*Abba*, Father!'" (Gal. 4:6). He prefers the high school musical to Broadway. He doesn't need us branded just the right way, saying all the catchphrases or wearing the right clothes. The truth is that most of us are thrift store shoppers trying to pretend we are fashionably sophisticated. It's exhausting. It isn't the life God wants for us.

What if I told you that there was a straightforward, organic approach to living for and loving God that didn't involve trends? That there was a sacred simplicity to this approach that allows us to breathe without fear of judgment or condemnation? A life that sees God as so much more than a life preserver to the drowning? Yes, he rescues us—but that's just the beginning of the story, not the end.

There is a braver and better approach that could and should become us after the storm, if only we will have the guts to follow the process to completion. It has proven to be timeless and has never failed a person or a generation. If you are willing to kick your assumptions to the curb, that Christianity is boring or rule-oriented, or that you are fine just the way you are, then an entirely different life is available. It is a life not driven by fear or worries, comfort or unhealthy cravings, pandemic or opinionated personalities. It is a process that begins, endures, and ends with *a perfect love that drives out fear*. It is a process that is a sacredly holistic prescription for living.

As with any process, the scope and sequence are vitally important. With some books, the reader may skip around, consuming content based on the interest of one chapter's focus versus another. This book is not that. Each chapter serves to build on the next. So, if you want the process to work, then let the process be . . . well . . . a process. In the following pages, I am letting our purpose in Jesus and the method described by Jesus lead to our best life in Jesus.

Purpose = Jesus

Process = Jesus' teachings

Product = Jesus' promise

In other words, our best life is found in the splendor of God's goodness through the pragmatic of daily living. As one of the most influential pastors in 1800 England described it: "Come and learn how to sing to the Lord a new song! Come and find peace, rest, joy, and all your souls can desire. Come and eat what is good and let your soul delight."[3]

A Warning about Dinosaurs

This is a book about choosing to live. We wake up every day with a choice to live today or lose today. It's fascinating that a failure to live well is a recipe for death. Quite unintentionally, so many of us plan our deaths with our daily routines. We have succumbed to survival, but surviving is just another form of dying, which brings us to a warning about dinosaurs.

To go through life just surviving is to miss the provision of God's enduring and transforming presence through all the ups and downs. It is to simply live like the dinosaurs. Theologian and author Leonard Sweet calls this survival approach to life "a dinosaurian philosophy":

> A dinosaurian philosophy of life is a basic brain response to everyday existence: feed on this, fight about that, protect yourself, and pleasure yourself as often as possible. And like the dinosaurs with their four rules of living— feeding, fighting, fleeing, and sex—we bring death and destruction to all around us as we ravage and ruin whatever we touch.[4]

We must fight the destructive desire to just survive. A person often becomes what they tolerate in their lives. For these ten steps to work, we must despise an illness that doesn't show up in blood work or X-rays. It is an ailment of the soul that leads to a despondent existence where faith, hope, and love seem to have gone on permanent holiday. While we have already labeled it as a "survival approach" and "dinosaurian philosophy," it is, quite sadly, the act of settling for mediocrity. What we will discover is a remedy to this illness that floods the soul with the light of God's goodness, allowing the teachings of Jesus to disinfect the decay of averageness.

Future Switch

The future is a canvas where God's grace offers you the opportunity to paint a masterpiece. And while many in the coming days may slide back into the slumber of a dinosaurian way of life, under the canvas of a blue tarp, there is an opportunity to switch that narrative around. That's right, you can capture and reimagine your future. "But what will this ten-step process produce?" one may ask.

Our aim is simple, sacred, and a bit mysterious. The process is designed to strip us down to the most organic version of self and then strive for a version of ourselves alive with purpose and possibility. I say it is mysterious because what God seeks to accomplish from one life to the next is completely his prerogative. The end goal is for each of us to discover the person we were meant to be all along—a person who is content with his or her journey. We can enjoy life and all that God offers in and through it, someone redeemed and living their best life in the present tense. And by "best life," I don't mean some self-help, prosperity around every corner, stick your head in the sand and forget the brokenness around you . . . type of life. No, what is meant by "best life" is fulfilling the idea of who God wants you to be. Or, as the Italians say, *la dolce vita*, meaning the sweet life or the good life. In this book, we search for the authentically good and sweet life that can only be experienced in Jesus.

There is a rhythm by which we are meant to live. It got lost long ago, and no algorithm on its best day can rediscover it. To do so, we must return to the words spoken by that renegade rabbi from Nazareth who taught, preached, and lived in such a magnetic manner for all generations to come. He knew we would be here standing in our front yards, overwhelmed by all that COVID-19 destroyed. He knew how we would feel and all the dark scenarios that would dance through our imaginations about the future. And so, he whispers down through the ages:

> "Come to me, all of you who are weary and burdened, and I will give you rest. Take up my yoke and learn from me, because I am lowly and humble in heart, and you will find rest for your souls. For my yoke is easy and my burden is light." (Matt. 11:28–30)

Here is the incredible thing about this invitation. Jesus isn't waiting for just the right time when you have repaired everything under the blue tarp covering your life. The thing about blue tarps is that there isn't anything impressive about them, and there isn't anything one can do to dress them up. It's a big, giant Band-Aid whose plastic veneer screams, "There is a lot that's broken under here!" Jesus wants you and all the pain, mistakes, regret, unhealthiness, loneliness, and anything else you've been covering up.

The very invitation of Jesus means it's okay to not be okay. . . .

But it also means that we get to keep company with and learn from Jesus.

And with Jesus, we discover the best life a human could ever be graced to experience.

God

Step 1: Create a Rhythm of Renewal

Beginnings

Beginnings Matter . . . A LOT

There is something very human about longing for a fresh beginning. I have experienced this on a very personal level. Beginnings are full of hope and possibility. The beginning is devoid of my past, which is littered with mistakes. It doesn't have a picture gallery of bad memories on constant display in my brain, and my emotions haven't devolved to a place of cynicism masked as criticism. Beginnings are pure and untainted. Beginnings provide a fresh canvas just waiting for the masterpiece to be revealed.

The beginning of any journey or process serves as both a starting point and a reference point. The inauguration of anything worth doing will also function as the foundation throughout the process of any endeavor. In our case, we are suggesting that our beginning allows us to start something new; it affords us the sacred opportunity to adopt a new way of thinking . . . a new way of living. The scope and sequence being put forth in the pages of this book are not subjective or theoretical in any way. This scope and sequence, this practical guide for your best life, has been tried and tested and approved by the highest authority in the universe. It cannot be over-stated that this is NOT simply a way of living. Rather, this is THE definitive manner in which we are to conduct ourselves, if we want our best life to be the end result.

Beginnings Are Important

And so, it is because of this that our discussion begins with God, who after all, begins his story with "In the beginning God" (Gen. 1:1). A purpose-filled scope and sequence of a life worth living must begin with the author of that life. For all humans, the author of human life is God. The psalmist explained it this way: "For it was you who created my inward parts; you knit me together in my mother's womb. I will praise you because I have been remarkably and wondrously made" (Ps. 139:13–14a). God also explained to the prophet Jeremiah that his future existence was known before he was ever conceived. In other words, God chose and knew Jeremiah before his conception. I mention the psalmist and Jeremiah here to make a very simple point: *our humanity was God's idea, he knew of us from eternity past, and, thus, our lives are sacred to him.* Since humanity was God's idea, then life itself is sacred and miraculous. Our beginning is sacred. Knowing our beginning point offers clarity, confidence, and comfort for the process ahead. How often do we know something is wrong or unhealthy or broken but lack the understanding of "how did I end up here"?

What if I told you the place we designate as "beginning" is actually the place that God wants us to put down roots and live. What if *the beginning* was really *the destination*? The greatest of all discoveries is the opportunity to find residence in the place of hope and potential, a beautiful space where fear and shame are irrelevant, a place where the future is as glorious as one can imagine. The place of beginning is God's best for us in this life. You see, God doesn't wait to give us his best, but he does wait until we are ready to receive his best. God is patient, wanting us to arrive at the place of beginnings. God's best is God's love toward a people who never asked for his love in the first place. Yet in our rebellion, he took the initiative to pursue us. And in his pursuit of us, we see the most loving act.

> The most loving act,
> God's best for us,
> the great initiative toward a people who so
>   easily forget,
> is Jesus on the cross.

This continues to make incredible sense as we follow the trajectory of God's story. If we look at the Bible as one big story, then it can be understood in four parts: creation, fall, redemption, and restoration. In short, God creates everything, including human beings as the crown of his creation, and places them in the garden. The garden is the original beginning. It was a place where everything was as it should be. If all of *the beginning* could be described in one word, that word would be *harmony*. Adam and Eve lived in harmony with each other, creation, and God himself. The beginning had no tainted past, no conflict, no fear, and no shame.

The beginning place was soon destroyed when the world's first couple listened to God's enemy. The enemy whispered a lie. Adam and Eve listened to the lie and allowed it to take root in their hearts and thoughts. In doing so, they rebelled against God and everything the garden represented. Their rebellion destroyed the harmony of this beautiful beginning place that had been created for them. In a moment, everything changed. NOTHING was as it should be.

In *The Jesus Storybook Bible*, Sally Lloyd-Jones summarized what happened next. In a few short sentences she captured the very heart of God's story from the fall to redemption, through the finished work of Jesus on the cross, to all things being restored and made new again:

> Before they left the garden, God made clothes for his children, to cover them. He gently clothed them and then sent them away on a long journey—out of the garden, out of their home. Well, in another story, it would all be over and that would have been . . . THE END. But not in this Story. God loved his children too much to let the story end there. Even though he knew he would suffer, God had a plan—a magnificent dream. One day, he would get his children back. One day, he would make the world their perfect home again. And one day, he would wipe every tear from their eyes.[1]

God's plan, from eternity past, was Jesus. God refused to allow rebellion to end with the rebellious. This is why every part of God's story really does whisper the name of Jesus. Jesus is God's way of getting us back to the beginning place. You see, the end of God's story brings us back to the beginning: grace.

The beauty of grace is that we are privileged to live in the place of beginnings. Sure, we age; our hair falls out or turns gray, or does a little of both. We wrinkle, our joints ache, and we become forgetful. Technology becomes a thing for "a younger generation," and we like our old gadgets just the way they are. The world spins on faster and faster as we begin to move a little slower. Seasons come and go, and with them we begin to lose loved ones. Little by little, life as we know it seems to take more than it gives. And yet, for those who have decided to live in the beginning place, even loss echoes hope. For loss is only an indication that we are getting closer to another part of this story. Living in the place of beginnings means . . .

> I experience God's best every day in a new and fresh way,
>
> his presence is as real and relevant as the day I crossed the line of faith,
>
> and even the sun bursts forth on the horizon, piercing the dark each day, as God's way of saying that his love is steadfast and his mercies are new every morning.

Since this is the case, then even the struggles of this life point me to the place where all things are forever made new. Our very decay points to a restored day, a day when all will be as it once was long ago in a garden . . . forevermore.

How to Live in the Beginning Place: Creating a Rhythm of Renewal

We must now ask ourselves a very important question: *How do we live in this place of beginnings, which has been made possible through the person and work of Jesus?* The beginning is where God desires us to live. It is a place, a life that doesn't take temporary reservations; there are no tourists, nor time-shares. Let's be clear: responsibility rests on the shoulders of every follower of Jesus to be accountable for the life we live.

A sad and often repeated story is that we are given freedom from sin and made new creations in Christ Jesus, but then we spend far too much energy wasting that freedom. Could you imagine an individual wasting away in a prison for some hor-rendous crime? There is no hope of parole or time reduced. This person's atrocities were so heinous that they will never breathe free air again. Now imagine that person being granted a complete pardon. And not only that, but a benefactor has offered them an incredible way to begin a new life through employment opportunities and housing, all in a city unfa-miliar with the person's past crimes. This person has every opportunity, through no merit of their own, to experience and live freedom every single day. But what if that person wasted the freedom by chasing their former life and, eventually, found themselves committing another crime that would compromise their freedom. It's as if they rebelled against the very opportu-nity given. The choice was to live free, or choose to live incon-sistently with the gift of freedom and suffer the consequences.

We, all of us, got ourselves kicked out of the garden. The creation narrative is the story of us. And yet, God made a way for us to begin again, to live in that beautiful place of beginnings, and all he asks of us is that we receive and pursue this newfound freedom. I believe there are four steps to establish a sense of rhythm renewal.

1. Choose God's Love

Each person has to make the decision for themselves to choose Jesus. At the beginning of Jesus' earthly ministry, following his baptism, he went into the wilderness to be tempted by the devil. After fasting for forty days and nights, he then endured a series of temptations all centered around Jesus' authority and worship. In the final portion of their discourse Jesus told him, "Go away, Satan! For it is written: Worship the Lord your God, and serve only him" (Matt. 4:10).

It's not surprising at all that this temptation occurred immediately following Jesus' baptism. How often do people receive the gift of salvation and get baptized, only to have significant temptation immediately thrown their way? We are all invited to the place of beginnings, but there will also be many invitations for us to leave. Therefore, there must be a consistent emphasis on choosing to worship the Lord our God. The gift of choice is a blessing that should never be underestimated or overlooked. Our response to God's love is to then choose to love God in return, and that means we are choosing to worship him. The gift of our salvation is that forever responding with adoration and obedience is a choice—a choice that only makes sense "in view of the mercies of God" (Rom. 12:1).

It is the last part of Jesus' statement to the devil that is most helpful. He says, *serve only him.* By choosing Jesus, we eliminate all other options to worship anything else. We are saying with our lives that there is only one true God, and we seek to worship him and him alone. When all other options for worship are eliminated in our lives, it affords us the ability to simply focus on our original purpose—the place of beginnings. By loving Jesus, we say, "Go away!" to any form of service divorced from honoring Jesus. Only the person confident in the grace of Jesus does not fall prey to worship false gods. After all, when we awaken to the person and work of Christ, we realize that there are no other gods that can be worshiped. In this sense, we could say that there are no false gods, just deceived people.

2. Recognize and Respond to God's Everyday Morning Reminder

My favorite time to be outside are those few minutes before a rainstorm builds. Living in central Florida gives me ample opportunity to enjoy those moments when the temperature drops, the wind begins to blow, and the sun seems to take a break. I will stop whatever I am doing and just go stand outside. It's as if nature itself is breathing in possibility. The air feels so fresh and clean against my face. Hope is on the move as the rain begins to fall. Spanish moss dances on the winds as they blow through the old oaks. The palm trees sway and those little ripples appear on the pond out front. If our little corner of cow country outside of Orlando, Florida, had a soundtrack, I would put the moments before a storm on repeat.

I love how God uses nature to whisper his purposes and presence. Each morning, the sun parades across the horizon and illuminates everything in its path. It awakens the world to a new day, one that has never been experienced before nor will it ever be experienced again. The prophet Jeremiah demonstrates this type of new beginning in the book of

Lamentations. Jeremiah had experienced more pain and disappointment in one life than others would in ten lifetimes. It is a book written by a brokenhearted man who spent many years sharing the message God had given him, only to have no one respond. That's right, zero response to God's message through his prophet Jeremiah. Furthermore, the city that he loved, Jerusalem, was being brutally overthrown. So the prophet put his laments, his sorrows, his pain, down on paper. It is such an emotional book that it caught the attention of one of history's most renowned artists, Rembrandt, who sought to depict it in his painting: *Jeremiah Lamenting the Destruction of Jerusalem*.

While reading the book, a section seems to burst forth from Jeremiah's soul, testifying to the character and goodness of God:

> Because of the LORD's faithful love
> we do not perish,
> for his mercies never end.
> They are new every morning;
> great is your faithfulness! (Lam. 3:22–23)

Jeremiah learned the secret of living in the beginning place, even when his entire life seemed littered with heartache and heartbreak. It was something to see about God in the dawning of each day. With every sunrise, just as the light covers the earth, we are covered in mercies of God. And guess what, it happens again and again without fail every morning. The lovingkindness of God is new every day. God puts on the most glorious light show every morning to remind us to reside in his faithfulness and experience his mercy.

God is inviting us to live in a place brimming with hope and breathing in possibility. That place that feels like the moments just before a storm, that space when the light pierces the darkness each morning, a place where we are new creations that will never grow old. The life you and I were meant to live revels in the beauty of grace, renewing our awe of God every day. For without awe and reverence for the Lord your God whose "mercies never end," life would be senseless, lacking any understanding or meaning.

Sure, there is pain, loss, and suffering in the beginning place. After all, we are redeemed but not yet restored. We are new creations here on the earth stumbling our way to heaven. But we are redeemed, we are new. Something has been granted to us that was lost in the garden. Therefore, God's enduring, unwavering, never-failing presence is our everyday, sustaining, keeping-us-new provision.

3. Plan for Daily Renewal

Once we have responded to God's love and awakened to the everyday reminder of grace, the foundation has been laid to create a plan. The need for a functioning plan in our lives cannot be overstressed. For our purposes, we want a plan that helps us to live in the beginning place, a plan that contributes to a rhythm of renewal. Redemption is something God accomplishes; renewal is something God gives us grace to pursue. We are all prone to entertain invitations that detract from and derail the life God wants for us. Thus, we need a plan that keeps us focused on seeking after the One who sought us first. A plan that includes:

Principles to Follow
*What specific beliefs will guide to a
rhythm of renewal?*

A Personalized Approach That Is Functional
How can a plan be customized to your season of life?

A Process That Facilitates
How will you measure goals, progress, and health needed for renewal?

A Purpose to Fulfill
What does the renewed life look like?

The "principles" are those guiding ideas that we follow. The "personalized approach" is customizing the plan to your uniqueness. The "process" is the practical manner that facilitates execution, and the "purpose" is the finished goal we seek to fulfill.

In any planning process, it is always good to begin with the end goal of the plan. What is it that the plan seeks to accomplish? The answer to that question allows us to plan with the end in mind and stay focused on the end goal throughout all steps of the plan. We move forward when we clearly know the finish line. In other words, our best life now (the present) is determined by our best life then (the end goal of the plan). So, to answer that question, let's now turn to one of the most practical statements Jesus made concerning how we live: "But seek first the kingdom of God and his righteousness, and all these things will be provided for you" (Matt. 6:33). This is one of those sentences that gets extracted in isolation and ends up getting printed on everything from coffee mugs to scented candles. Now, I'm not throwing shade on merchandising, but the strength of this rule for living is found in taking a little deeper look than just the oft-tweeted portion. So, light a candle and grab your coffee mug because there is so much to be gleaned in this short declaration.

First, the *seek first* verse comes in the second portion of Jesus' Sermon on the Mount, his most extensive sermon recorded by any of the gospel writers. This amazing verse is not an island, but part of the mainland of spiritual principles guiding Christians in true righteousness. Preaching to a Jewish audience, Jesus is positioned as "the new Moses,"[2] sharing God's message to an audience who felt intimately connected to the audience who would have looked to Moses for leadership. The parallel between Moses and Jesus shows the length to which God will go to enlighten. God wanted the Jewish people to see and understand; he, likewise, wants us to understand true righteousness.

Let us also understand that, just as the sun rises each day illuminating the earth, so we rise each day seeking to be enlightened all the more in righteousness. Not to get too sophisticated, but the verb *seek* is written in the present imperative tense in the Greek language, meaning whatever is said is a command in the present and future. Followers of Jesus should be the most curious people on the planet because they rise with the seekers' desire to know Jesus all the more. We are to seek—and to go on seeking—all that it means to live new in the grace of Jesus every day. As one scholar put it: "Grace kindles the desire and keeps it ever active in this life."[3]

Finally, while I love that the *seek first* verse appears in the larger context of the Sermon on the Mount, it becomes even more practical that it appears in a section dealing with worry and anxiety. The key to a worry-free life is a singular focus.

The words of Jesus atop a mountain overlooking the Sea of Galilee echo down through the ages, bidding us to give up our pursuit for survival. Survival is a dangerous game we were never intended to play. And yet, it is a trap we so easily fall into. And more years only makes it more complicated. It's almost like the more birthday candles we have to blow out, the more fires we are trying to put out in our lives. The more we have that concerns us, the more concerned we become. "How am I going to get a job, pay the bills, find a spouse, keep my marriage healthy, choose a college, pay off college debt, and send my kids to college!?!" On and on it goes, and the whole time, Jesus is saying, "Consider the birds of the sky: They don't sow or reap or gather into barns, yet your heavenly Father feeds them. Aren't you worth more than they?" (Matt. 6:26).

Since you are more valuable than a bird, take heart that the God who created you has made a commitment to you. You are free to be curious and keep on seeking Jesus. God has taken care of the hard part; we don't have to worry. Just create a plan—a plan guided by the principles of Scripture, personalized to who you are, with a clear process, that enables you to fulfill the purpose of living in the beginning place. God redeems and will give grace to those who plan on renewal.

4. Practice Achieving God's Present Wants

God doesn't always get his way in the here and now. I know that may seem like an off-the-wall crazy statement at first glance, but consider this: we live in a broken world where redemption is possible, but we are awaiting that universe-shaking moment when God will restore and make all things new. Even while living in a fallen world where we are redeemed but not yet restored, God has desires for his people. The season of redemption offers us so many incredible opportunities, many of which hinge on our obedience.

Therefore, the last step in a life that enjoys a rhythm of renewal is seeking out those opportunities to fulfill God's desires in the here and now. A life seeking happiness and contentment based on *What would my life look like if I received everything I desire?* will only lead to disappointment. On the other hand, the person who dares to let their life be a response to *What would it look like if God's desires were met through my life's journey?* will live renewed because they are pleasing God. A life given away to the service of God is never wasted.

In the coming chapters we are going to look at the very practical necessary steps for engaging God and others well. Yet, all that will be discussed only works when we have made the decision to live renewed. In other words, this rhythm of renewal affords us the opportunity to live the best possible version of our lives in the here and now. Before moving on, we need an image in our heads of how Jesus' love and his patience guide us to the beginning place.

Rocking Chair

When I think of God's patient pursuit of his people, I often think of a rocking chair. I know that may seem like a strange image, but let me explain. Jesus spent a lot of time telling stories all about God's love and how he takes initiative to love his people. One of my favorites—okay, maybe my all-time favorite—is the story that has been historically referred to as "the prodigal son" or "the lost son." You can read about it in Luke 15:11–32, but I like to imagine it unfolded like this:

There once was a very beautiful family. The father worked hard but was very kind to his employees. He was the type of man who only knew one speed. He was an all-or-nothing kind of leader, and it paid off for him over the years. His business was a family farm that seemed to thrive with the coming and going of each season. Though many factors, both social and economic, contributed to the Jewish custom of marriage at that time in history, his marriage to his wife was one blessed with love.

Early in their love story, she would serve the business by fulfilling a multiplicity of roles. This meant, at times, caring for the finances, while other times, it meant helping feed the household and its workers. Her favorite task was that of planning the annual banquet to celebrate another blessed year of success on the farm from harvest to healthy flocks. It really was an elaborate event that brought everyone who contributed to the business together. It was a party that lasted for days. There was amazing meat, wine, music, and dancing. The household was filled with joy, laughter, and gratitude. It was a time when the husband and wife celebrated with all the workers. For those few days each year, everyone was celebrated and the amount of happiness one experienced wasn't based on their role or station on the farm. Each man and woman danced and feasted as friends who had accomplished something special together.

As time passed, this couple entered a new season of life. Their firstborn son was everything they could have hoped for in a child. As he grew, so did his interest in all things with the family business. One day, he would be with the sheepherders asking questions and pretending to be older than he actually was. Another day, he would be found in the fields harvesting wheat. He felt that the vast farmland his family owned was a world to itself. Being mesmerized by possibility, his potential for taking his father's place took shape. Without any official announcement, he simply became his father's apprentice. It was a blessed season indeed.

Harvests came and went and then another blessing came to this already happy household in the form of another son. Born healthy, this second son was born with an innate sense of adventure. While the first son thought the family farm was the world, the second was always looking beyond their borders to another world. When he became a teenager, he looked for any reason to travel. He would fulfill the assignments and tasks his father assigned, but the family business never became his passion. So much so, that he began to look at the annual banquets and everything in between with a skepticism that eventually turned to disdain. Nevertheless, seasons would come and go, and the second son felt trapped.

Through it all, his mother demonstrated a calm patience. She possessed that special gift of steadfast maternal love, a force more powerful than almost anything else in the universe. Her love kept the second son grounded. And when the storms raged inside of him, only she had the ability to calm the crashing waves. Her heart was in tune with his pain, and her presence somehow lightened the weight of his struggles and baggage.

There are days when our words are inadequate to convey the description of our emotions. These are moments in life with only our tears accompany us through the seconds, minutes, and hours ahead. Such was the day when the husband lost the love of his life, and two sons had to say goodbye to their mother. An unwelcomed sickness caused her body to deteriorate quickly. With family by her side, even the parting words seemed too rushed.

A dark cloud seemed to settle over the family farm. To her mourning husband, every inch of the business they had built together seemed to echo memories. Days turned into weeks, weeks into seasons, and with the passing of time the once joyful farm now endured rather than enjoyed the days. There were no more annual festivals, causing the work to feel all the more laborious. Things eventually did begin to improve. But no matter how much life progressed, the festivals never returned. The father attempted to demonstrate his appreciation in other ways. He gave more to his employees, and the gentle word of encouragement for a long day's work was now the new normal.

Though his heart would never completely mend, the father was on the road to a new normal. And then, another bombshell arrived. There are some days that leave a lasting imprint on our minds, and no matter how hard we try, the memory can never be erased. Such was the day when the father's youngest son brought to him a heartbreaking request. The son wanted to receive his inheritance now rather than waiting for his father's death. It was a rock-bottom moment. First his beloved wife, now his second-born son.

The father always knew the farm was of little incentive to his son, but he never would have imagined a day such as this. To the casual onlooker, it appeared that the son had such a longing for life beyond the farm, that he was willing to go to any lengths to experience it. Even wishing his father was dead. Maybe it was because so much had already been lost, maybe he was just too broken. Nevertheless, the father acquiesced the unholy request and off the youngest went, chasing a life he had only imagined.

Shortly thereafter, the father officially passed the baton of leadership to his firstborn son, and retired. But instead of enjoying the fruit of his life's work, he chose a different path. He chose to honor God who had so richly blessed his farm, he chose to honor his wife who had relentlessly loved him, and he chose to fight for the soul of a wayward son. He didn't know where his son had gone, so he chose to fight the only way he could. Each day he sat on his front porch in a rocking chair. And each day, he said a simple prayer as he stared down the one road leading off his property:

> Father above,
> please hear this father's care,
> my son is lost to himself and only you know
>   where.
> Bring him home as soon as you can,
> bring him home that I may hold him again.

Some days he whispered the prayer over and again as he stared off into the distance. Other times he would pray it once and spend the rest of the day rocking and reflecting on all the good memories. Months of rocking turned into years. The father's health began to deteriorate, and some days, he needed assistance getting in and out of his rocking chair. At times, his firstborn son tried to distract him. To the firstborn, his father was wasting away, hoping for a day that would never come.

It was a normal day deep in that season of the year when the rains rarely fall. Every time the wind would blow, little dust tornadoes would dance across the landscape. The various herds could be seen across the rolling hills and the barns were full with grain from last season's harvest. One of the farmhands helped the patriarch to his usual perch, promising to return soon to check on him.

Once the father was alone, he began to slowly rock while looking down the road ahead. As he had prayed thousands of times before, he began to utter those oft repeated but never routine words: "Father above, please hear this father's care, my son—" In that moment, he interrupted himself. A figure had appeared on the dusty horizon. The father's failing mind refused, at first, to believe its familiarity. *Maybe it is a wounded sojourner who has lost his way?* he thought. The figure seemed to limp along rather than walk, and his head hung low like someone defeated by the harshness of life. He dismissed the thought as soon as it formulated in his brain.

Hope began to spring up inside him like never before. And almost involuntarily, he stood to his feet and began to run. Heart pounding, scarcely enough energy to breathe, he ran as fast as his aging legs would allow. With each stride, his belief was renewed with an even deeper sense of astonishment and love.

> He was "filled with compassion. He ran, threw his arms around his neck, and kissed him."
>
> The son said to him, "Father, I have sinned against heaven and in your sight. I'm no longer worthy to be called your son."
>
> But the father told his servants, "Quick! Bring out the best robe and put it on him; put a ring on his finger and sandals on his feet.

> Then bring the fattened calf and slaughter it,
> and let's celebrate with a feast, because this
> son of mine was dead and is alive again; he
> was lost and is found!" So, they began to cel-
> ebrate. (Luke 15:20–24)

It had been years since the smells, sights, and sounds of
the festivals had permeated the family's home at the center of
the farm. The father's capacity to celebrate life had been so
diminished by the loss of his wife. And now, in a moment's
time, a prayer had been answered. There was reason to celebrate because life had returned in the most glorious fashion.
It was like the frigid chill of winter was suddenly lifted and the
springtime burst forth from the home. The son was home and,
with him, all the possibilities of what once was.

Many times, I have read the story and seen myself in it.
The lost son chased a life he was never intended to experience,
only to discover his home was where he was loved. But the
more I read the story of the lost son, and maybe the older I
get, the more I think it is a story of a father waiting, longing,
loving from a distance, and refusing to give up. I think that is
how God is with us. He is waiting, wanting, and steadfastly
loving us. In fact, God doesn't wait to give us his best. He
offers us the very road to forgiveness.

The story of the lost son is dramatic, but not for the reasons I formerly thought. Sure, if it were a Rated R movie, it
would be for the son's rebellious activity to spend all his money
on fleshly desires. But the true drama, the part that would
bring tears to your eyes, is that of a father in a rocking chair
uttering a heartfelt prayer day after day. And when the son
appears on the horizon, tears would stream down our faces just

as they do the father's. In other words, we would resonate most with the father's love.

The desire for "something else" is as old as time. We see it in the garden with Adam and Eve. We see it in Luke's Gospel with the story of the lost son. But in every case, God gives us his best in the beginning, and in so doing, invites us to reside in the beginning place. We are prone to wander in all the wrong directions, but when we decide to wander home, we find that love has been waiting on us the entire time. We discover that we didn't need to leave the beginning place to go on a journey or find a more fulfilling experience. The beginning place is where we reside in life's journey, and it has everything we could ever need and more. Since God gives us his best in the beginning by placing us *in Christ*, then there is nothing better beyond. So, the decision to reside and create a rhythm in the beginning place is a choice that brings focus to all other choices. And an old-fashioned rocking chair just might be an image that helps us remember home is with Jesus, and for some of us . . . Jesus is waiting.

The love of Jesus will guide you to the beginning place, and his grace is sufficient enough to keep all of us there. But while his grace is sufficient, it also serves as the greatest of motivations for us to do our part. We are prone to drift, so we have to win the battle in our lives every day to listen to the right voice. It's the voice of our heavenly Father who whispers his love for us on every page of the Scriptures, and in each painted sky or glorious starlit night. As the late Rev. Ralph Spaulding Cushman once penned:

> I never climb my hilltop
> But I find that God is there,

Nor watch the windblown clouds,
but that
His voice is in the air.

I know I cannot see His face
Nor touch a warming hand,
But God is on my hilltop,
And there's glory in the land.[4]

In this chapter, I have attempted to paint a picture that shows how God offers his best to us, Jesus, in the beginning. And because he offers his best right out of the gate, we are then invited to live our lives in that beginning place. It is not a place divorced from pain or problems, but it is a place filled with the presence of our Savior. This is why we can confidently cling to the idea that *God's provision for our lives is God's presence in our lives.* The preceding thoughts have sought to convey the spirit in which we should live our lives. The entire idea of "the beginning place" mirrors the narrative that is the Bible, particularly focusing on the creation narrative and redemption. The late J. I. Packer, who impacted millions through his writing ministry with such classics as *Knowing God,* penned it this way:

> Creation and covenant together give God a double claim on our obedience. The claim springs, you might say, from both paternity (fatherhood in the sense of creatorship) and matrimony (the covenant relationship).[5]

Image

Step 2: Give Up and Chase the Light

There was once a marvelous and odd flower that grew in a garden. It was bright and full of life. It was marvelous because its personality and colors burst forth into the sky each day like a shooting star. It was odd because it exuded a behavior that seemed strange to all the other flowers in the garden. You see, all the other florae pretty much remained motionless throughout the day, with the exception of the occasional breeze. Throughout the garden was an array of colors, each unique in and of itself. But one flower's uniqueness stood out among the rest, and it was all because of a peculiar, magnificent, odd mannerism that set it apart. While beauty was beholden to the unique color of each plant's immovable convictions, this one seemed to make a strange sort of motion throughout the day.

All the flowers thought some defect or dysfunction must bear the blame for such eccentric behavior. To them, they could not understand why such a verdure would waste its energy and, thus, its life by constantly moving throughout the day. *Doesn't this odd individual sense its social standing being stained by such hullabaloo?* all the other flowers thought.

Then, one day, a shrub whose roots had long since taken deep into the soil, dared to ask: "Uhhhh, say you over there, what is all the strangeness that seems to consume your days? Don't you know that it is quite uncivilized for greenery such as us?" The odd and marvelous flower had never thought of how others perceived it, nor what was proper floral etiquette. Still, a response was given to the question asked: "Why, I am chasing the sun?"

"You will never catch the sun, so why on earth are you chasing it!" the shrub abruptly replied.

"I said I was chasing the sun. I never said I was trying to catch it. You see, I chase the sun to catch the light. I am a giant sunflower, designed to follow the arch of the sun every day. And in so doing, I catch the light and soak up its rays."

"Hmmm," the shrub replied in a confused way, "well, it's still hullabaloo."

I don't think any plant in the entire garden ever understood the sunflower. It was meant to stand out among the rest. It reached out for as much light and life as could be experienced every single day. Still, her uniqueness didn't confine her. Rather, it defined her as marvelous and odd . . . and there is nothing wrong with being both.

You . . . me . . . we are all marvelous and odd, or just marvelously odd! We were created to rise each day and chase the sun, following its arch and catching as much light as can be experienced in any given day. Never forget that! God has given a gift, one that "other flowers in the garden" may not understand. We also realize that, at times, a cloud can block out the light, causing you to feel frustrated and confused. But take heart, you are a giant sunflower, for the sun never goes away . . . and soon, the clouds will pass by.

I think out of all the plants and flowers, the giant sunflower best captures the life we were created for. We are a people called out of darkness and into the marvelous light of Jesus. The great change in us, our miraculous transformation, leaves us clearly believing that only Jesus deserves our worship. If step one of your best life is discovering the beginning place and creating a rhythm of renewal for living there, then step two is to understand that you were meant to chase the light. Let's dive into a practical guide of a singular focus giving worshipful affection to only Jesus.

First, we must wrestle with those things that receive the love and affection only meant for Jesus: idols. An *idol* is something we imagine to be more important than God, or it is when we imagine God to be something he is not. J. I. Packer worded it this way: "'This is how I like to think of God' should ever be trusted. An imagined God will always be quite imaginary and unreal."[1] Idols are the anti-God substitutes that seek to capture your affection and love. Idols threaten the very soul of life itself. We cannot live in the beginning place and worship anything other than Jesus. The notion of idols and Jesus cohabitating makes about as much sense as light and dark sharing the same space; it is impossible.

As one theologian put it: "Idolatry substitutes the thing for the person. The very essence of idolatry is that it is the worship of a thing instead of the worship of a person; the dead idol has taken the place of the living God."[2] And the "thing" can come in all shapes, sizes, forms, and images. We can idolize possessions like cars and houses. It can be status and/or money, relationships or social media influence, health or style, and the list could just go on and on. You see, whatever is most important to us is our god. And the challenge that so many of us have is that we sing songs on Sunday about God's importance, but in the end, they are hollow of any meaning because a simple reflection on the lives we live proves something other than the God we sing about is more important. If God is an interruption or a side function, then something else in your life has taken his place.

Avoid the Siren's Song

It would seem that the two biggest idols in our world today are "power" and "popularity." This probably doesn't come as much of a surprise. In fact, it appears that the pandemic of 2020 only magnified humanity's desire to accumulate more power and more popularity. And yet, it is historically fascinating that the beginning years of the church consisted of a tribe of people with no power and certainly no popularity. Let that sink in for a moment. An outlawed group of people following the teachings of a rabbi from a remote city, whom they believed to be the Messiah, changed the world while the largest empire in human history stood in direct opposition. Eventually, Constantine would decriminalize Christian worship, following his own conversion, in AD 313. Nevertheless, well over a hundred years before Constantine ever came to power, a Christian scholar and apologist named Tertullian penned: "the blood of the martyrs is the seed of the Church." I mention this to highlight one simple historical truth: that while Christianity has, at times, enjoyed favor from governments and empires, *our faith has enjoyed its greatest seasons of flourishment and growth during times of heavy persecution.*

Power

If greatness is your goal, then power will be your downfall.

There is a lie that has infected society. It's subtle and is slowly penetrating the whole of culture until, at last, it becomes an assumed norm. This untruth is as old as "your eyes will be opened and you will be like God" (Gen. 3:5). The lie is that we were destined to be great and powerful, a dominating force that accomplishes stuff through our strength and might. The apostle Paul warns of this in the strongest terms: "Be careful that no one takes you captive through philosophy and empty deceit based on human tradition, based on the elements of the world, rather than Christ" (Col. 2:8). The philosophy that Paul refers to is false teaching that originated with human beings, as opposed to the gospel which is from God—a power struggle contrived by humans in an effort to achieve power they were never intended to possess by espousing a message that is greater than the gospel. This lie was believed by Adam and Eve. It is the lie that Paul was writing against with Colossian believers, who believed that if you pursue greatness . . . then you will be more.

The illusion of power always promises more—significance, more possessions, more authority, more influence . . . more and more and more. But in the end, it is "empty deceit." It is a lie. That is why pursuing greatness leads to a power that ultimately will be your downfall. It is empty and hollow. Idolatry is always built on lies, and power is no exception. Greatness is reserved for the One who even "the heavens declare the glory of God" (Ps. 19:1). After all, "the LORD is great . . . his greatness is unsearchable" (Ps. 145:3). Pursue God, not greatness. Jesus warned us that power isn't our purpose: "On the contrary, whoever wants to become great among you must be your servant" (Matt. 20:26). He even uses himself as the ultimate example of humble servitude teaching "the Son of Man did not come to be served, but to serve, and to give his life as a ransom for many" (v. 28). Think about that for a moment. Jesus is God; he has all authority in heaven and earth. We could never begin to fathom his greatness and power. Yet, he shows us the path forward is to never bow to the idol of power, but to kneel in humble service and sacrifice.

Popularity

When popularity is your idol, then life becomes a staged and false narrative.

The desire to be liked is exhausting. It's like a drug that numbs our senses to what it means to be authentically human. The pursuit of popularity causes us to wear a mask of a fictional character. We want everyone to believe we are actually someone we were never intended to be. It's a phantom version of self we are acting out, hoping to fool the audience. Posing just right, cropping out the unwanted, filtering the original to manipulate our flaws and environment. Carefully crafted stories, dances choreographed to be funny or sexually suggestive, and opinions are shared in an effort to prove our "wokeness." Yet in the end, when no one is watching, we can't even breathe without wondering if someone cares. Social media and screens have, for so many, simply become a mask we wear on a stage to create a false narrative.

A few years ago, I struggled with chronic pain. Working a series of manual labor jobs where I didn't lift heavy things correctly, along with a couple of car accidents, had caught up with me in the form of a neck fracture. Oh, and enough bone spurs to fill an X-ray. I would wake up in the morning, take a breath, and then have pain shoot from my neck all the way down to the tips of my fingers on my left arm. Every time I saw my doctor, he informed me that surgery was necessary at some point, and then he prescribed me something for the pain. I constantly traded between over-the-counter and prescription-strength pain medications. On one particular visit, I told him that the medicine wasn't working anymore. He said, "Well, there are obviously some stronger medications I could prescribe, but they will only mask your pain. I advise you to have the surgery and deal with the cause of your pain before you create permanent damage to your neck." Not wanting to go down the path of "stronger meds," which would only delay the inevitable, I complied and scheduled the surgery.

I believe our pursuit of popularity masks a much deeper problem. So often we take the route of more and stronger meds to mask the pain. We utilize more platforms, outperform previous posts, and try to associate our narratives with other fictional characters. The occasional person may become a "public figure" with the library of content they create. But most of the time the pursuit leaves us feeling alone and unfulfilled. That's because God didn't create us to wear masks.

God doesn't want you to find your significance in views, likes, comments, subscribers, or followers. Social platforms are awesome tools for communicating, networking, keeping up with friends, and don't forget those hilarious memes and videos. But it is a terrible place to discover your self-worth. It is a place where the desire to be liked is actually motivated by a poor self-image and self-esteem. Hence, we mask our insecurities in the relentless and hollow pursuit of approval.

Now I know we seek popularity through a multiplicity of avenues; I simply reference social platforms because they have become the dominant manner through which we communicate. In any case, it's time to take the masks off, kick the fictional version of yourself to the curb, and abandon the quest to stage everything just right. Remember, you "have been remarkably and wondrously made" (Ps. 139:14) and your self-worth has been forever established in Jesus.

I wonder how many times we strive to create a brand and a platform, to accumulate likes and influence . . . only to then turn around and say, "Look what God did." What if, and I'm just spitballing here, God preferred a version of the current you without all the filters and editing? What if a more organic you, perhaps a less popular and powerful version, is the clay he seeks to mold? But—and here is a real head-scratcher—what happens if we've become shaped and emboldened by a version of self that was predetermined and prepackaged by a popularity-seeking, power-hungry society?

You see, the biggest challenge for some is to realize that, like in Homer's *Odyssey*, we listened to Sirens serenading from afar. Sirens were creatures in Greek mythology who enticed sailors to their destruction with an alluring song. As in the *Odyssey*, modern-day Sirens of society sing songs of power and popularity that promise so much and deliver so little. In our post-pandemic culture, the song itself has become a form of idolatry. Its melody catches our attention, but its lyrics are hollow in their promise for significance. In the end, popularity and power leave us unsatisfied and simply hungry for more.

The song of idolatry is like taking a drink, only to discover you are thirstier than when you first lifted the glass to your lips. It is a pathway to fear of what could be lost, pressure to maintain a pirated knockoff version of self, and a posture to worship all the wrong things. This is a version of self that can be found on the shelf, right next to a thousand other replicates. It lacks all the originality its veneer projected. And yet, this song of idolatry is the soundtrack to so many lives. For all it projects and promises, it leaves one shipwrecked and broken against the rocks near the shore. We are left broken by the expectations of others and broken by the expectations we place upon ourselves. It's false hope at the furthest depth of hopelessness. "The real horror of idols is not merely that they give us nothing, but that they take away from us even that which we have."[3]

For all who have listened to the song and steered your ship toward the sirens, who have drunk from that cup, you don't have to remain broken. You can give up the endless search to display a version of yourself with which you aren't even happy. The soundtrack of the past doesn't have to determine the song of the future. So, what do you do?

It begins with giving up.

You read those words correctly. Give up on being exhausted by energy wasted on wasted time. Give up on the cancerous focus that was dedicated to comparison. Give up on bowing down to a replicated veneered version of existence. Give up listening to the white noise of a societal song that overpromises and never delivers. Give up. That's where it begins. Just come to that place in the journey, the honest place, where one realizes that the idols that have been elevated in life never edify.

The honest place where we come face-to-face with the farce of pretending to be someone else.

The best part of the honest place is that it is also the place of awakening to a truth once lost. It is here that you can take the broken pieces and discover acceptance. To honestly approach God is the starting point to discovering all that God desires for your life. To take the broken pieces of our lives and give them to Jesus, is the beginning of pure amazement. It is the beginning of not having to live up to . . . *whatever*, and becoming defined by the most awesome love in the universe. Jesus doesn't make brokenness better; he makes it beautiful. That's the miracle.

Recognize the Gods That Aren't

Once we have recognized the wastefulness of listening to the siren song of idolatry . . . once we give up . . . then we are positioning ourselves to be the worshiper that God intended us to be. Never give worshipful affection to someone or something that can't forgive your sins. When we chase the light, we then choose to have our image daily determined and identified by Jesus. Also, when we chase the light, we are making a statement with our lives about "the gods that aren't."

Whether your idol is power, popularity, or something else, true worship is never found when a knee is bent to anything or anyone other than Jesus. That image is self-defeating and limiting. Let's consider it this way: an idol is a false god. It is a version of god that is a lie, yet we give it the attention that was intended for God. If it is a "version" of god, then it was contrived and created by human beings. Human beings are limited creatures, in that they were created by a Creator who is limitless. Since "limitlessness lies at the heart and center of the nature of God,"[4] anything that is limited should not be worshiped. A god that is contrived and created is no god after all. So, in this sense, we could say that there are no false gods, only deceived individuals.

And now we arrive at a most important reality: *worship only makes sense and is correct when we have a right understanding of God.* Because God is spiritual in nature, our worship must be spiritual as well. The healthier our view of God becomes, the more capacity we have to worship him. And the more we worship him, the more the image of our lives looks like Jesus.

Awaken to the Nature of Worship

Probably the most helpful event in Jesus' ministry, on the subject of worship, is his conversation with the Samaritan woman in John 4. One of my favorite things about Jesus is that he makes a priority of those whom the rest of the world views as outcasts. He makes divine appointments with those discarded by culture. The woman he met with at the well fit the category of discarded and unwelcomed.

As the world was spinning round and round two thousand years ago, Jesus kept a divine appointment sitting by a well at high noon to rescue a lonely outcast. Their conversation revolved around the nature of worship (vv. 20, 23–26):

> **The Samaritan woman:** "Our ancestors worshiped on this mountain, but you Jews say that the place to worship is in Jerusalem."

Jesus: "An hour is coming, and is now here, when the true worshipers will worship the Father in Spirit and in truth. Yes, the Father wants such people to worship him. God is spirit, and those who worship him must worship in Spirit and in truth."

The Samaritan woman: "I know that the Messiah is coming" (who is called Christ). "When he comes, he will explain everything to us."

Jesus: "I, the one speaking to you, am he."

It is obvious she has a great deal of confusion concerning both the where and the who of worship. One group says this mountain is the place to worship, others say it's that distant city. Jesus methodically navigates the conversation away from the place of worship to the nature of worship. In doing so, he answers the question that everyone should ask about worship: What is God looking for? Worship should never be a guessing game, so Jesus makes it crystal clear: *the place of your worship is infinitely less important than the focus of your worship being on the person and work of Jesus.* Since God is limitless, then worship to him cannot be confined to a location.

To worship in spirit and truth requires a focus on Jesus, for he is the light of the world and offers the clarity we need. So, what is meant by the word *worship*? We've already seen that Jesus takes the guessing game out of worship. But, while worship is not ambiguous, it is mysterious. Think about it this way: the Bible teaches that God is love, light, and spirit. God isn't tangible, you cannot measure or contain him. Yet he is

Inspected By: Ahide_Hernandez

**Sell your books at
sellbackyourBook.com!**
Go to sellbackyourBook.com
and get an instant price
quote. We even pay the
shipping - see what your old
books are worth today!

knowable, he is truth, and he sent Jesus to take up residence with us so we could find our way back. Eugene Peterson's *The Message* explains this in an artful yet practical manner:

> The Word became flesh and blood,
>   and moved into the neighborhood.
> We saw the glory with our own eyes,
>   the one-of-a-kind glory,
>   like Father, like Son,
> Generous inside and out,
>   true from start to finish. (John 1:14 MSG)

Or to say it another way: "Christ is the only perfect visible Image of the one perfect invisible God and therefore can be the only Object of worship by one who has been redeemed into God's family."[5] Our understanding of worship must then include the entirety of the redeemed existence responding to all that is known of the Redeemer.[6] Worship is then *an expression whereby a redeemed individual bows down before the Redeemer through both attitude and action.* So, the question we must always be asking ourselves is: Did the posture of my heart and the practice of my hands demonstrate allegiance to the person of Jesus?

Furthermore, Jesus said of worship "an hour is coming, and is now here" (John 4:23), meaning worship is to be done in the present moment and in the present place. The expression of our worship takes many forms: singing, service, being a part of a church family, Bible study, prayer, evangelism, doing one's work for the glory of God, loving family and others well, and the list could literally go on and on. Yes, there is a multiplicity of ways we worship, but there should also be a conviction as to the present-tense continuity of our worship.

Wherever we go, he is there
Whatever we do, should be done to his care

Whenever we live, let it be in his name
However it goes, must point always to his fame[7]

Awakening to a worship-filled life is like breathing clean air for the first time after a lifetime of inhaling smog, like being numb and then one day experiencing all five senses. It is both a short and long trip from false gods and the siren's songs to faithfulness and the Savior's way. A life full of worship has emerged from the shadows of deadness to the glory of God's grace. Worship is our *purpose*; it is what informs all the other purposes of our lives.

This chapter is titled "Image," which I realize is a term that can be misconstrued as self-consumed, but we all have an image. We are all physical beings living in a created world. If we seek to live well in a post-pandemic world, then the image of our lives should more and more reflect the love of God. We are image-bearers who have been redeemed and, therefore, should project the inward reality of what Christ has accomplished. A healthy image is discovered, cultivated, and deepened as we grow in our worship.

The pandemic of 2020/21 took a lot from us. It stripped us down, exposing some good, but also exposing a darkness that was lying just beneath the surface for so long. Some days, we wondered if the better angels of our nature had gone on a permanent vacation. The images projected on glowing screens everywhere painted a dim and dismal picture of pain and unrest. Assumptions that had long been held of problems solved turned out to be misleading myths. We have to decide: Do we want the comfort of a false narrative

. . . or would we rather create a new redemptive story? If the redemptive story option resonates with your soul, then being an authentic worshiper of God positions you to write it. Give up and chase the light.

Words

Step 3: Let the Word Shape Your Words

On the night of June 17, 2015, evil darkened the door of Mother Emanuel AME Church.

Though it often goes by its shortened name, Mother Emanuel, the full name is Emanuel African Methodist Episcopal (A.M.E.) Church. It is a church with a long, rich history and purpose, and belongs to a denomination of equal historical significance. The A.M.E., conceived in 1816, is the first independent Protestant denomination founded by black Christians. It is a denomination that did not begin over theological differences with other denominations. Rather, its founder, Rev. Richard Allen, sought an environment where people of African descent would be esteemed with civil and human rights. It is important to remember that the notion of dignity for all church members is what gave birth to the A.M.E.

Mother Emanuel would be founded in South Carolina, in 1817, when the denomination was only a year old, thus becoming the first black congregation in the South to be a part of the first black denomination. Throughout its history, Mother Emanuel would be a lightning rod for different reasons. For example, in response to Nat Turner's slave rebellion, the city of Charleston outlawed all black congregations. This caused the church to meet in secret from 1834 until the end of the Civil War in 1865. One of the long-standing traditions in the church was that the senior pastor would also aspire to political office as an effort to keep the needs of the community a priority. The denomination's original motto was "God our Father, Christ our Redeemer, Man our Brother."

In 2015, Rev. Clementa Carlos Pinckney was the senior pastor of Mother Emanuel and served as a state senator. His friends called him "Clem." After campaigning for the Democratic party earlier in the day, Pinckney showed up that evening for Bible study. The text being studied that night was Mark 4 and the parable of the seed sower. Around 8:00 p.m., a twenty-one-year-old homegrown terrorist was parking his Hyundai in the mostly empty lot outside Mother Emanuel. He slipped in a side door and made his way down to the basement, where twelve parishioners had gathered. At 8:06 p.m. he awkwardly appeared and was immediately welcomed into the Bible study. He spent about an hour with the community before he pulled out a handgun and began his murderous rampage.

He began with Pinckney and, after that, there seemed to be no sadistic logic to which victims would be killed. Pinckney was just forty-one years old. The other victims were Cynthia Hurd, fifty-four; Tywanza Sanders, twenty-six; Sharonda Singleton, forty-five; Myra Thompson, fifty-nine; Ethel Lance, seventy; Susie Jackson, eighty-seven; the Rev. Daniel Simmons Sr., seventy-four; and DePayne Doctor, forty-nine. The ages of the Emanuel 9, as they are often referred to, ranged from mid-twenties to late-eighties. But in some somber way, their ages really didn't matter, nor did their theology or any other descriptor we could come up with . . . save one. Dylann Roof murdered nine people in cold blood simply because they were black. A police document reports that he made racially inflammatory remarks when shooting his victims.[1]

As details emerged regarding this young white supremacist, one thing became clearer with each discovery.: this was a man full of hate. All his posted comments, manifesto, pictures, and even a website he created painted a picture of an individual so engrossed with hate that racial prejudice seeped from his very pores. But bullets and blood, martyrs and massacre, would not be the end of the story of Mother Emanuel or her people. Hate never gets the last word, nor does it determine how the story will end.

The A.M.E. Church had been founded on dignity. And when the unspeakable happened, those who were most hurt acted with such dignity that it left a nation realizing: *theirs was not just a historical faith, but a living one.* Shortly after Roof was arrested, he made his first appearance in court. While the perpetrator stood shackled, appearing on a video monitor, in the actual court room sat the family members and loved ones of those whose lives he had so quickly snuffed out. Each family member was given the opportunity to speak to Dylann Roof directly. Nadine Collier, the daughter of seventy-year-old Ethel Lance, was one of the first to share. Looking into a video monitor at the face of the twenty-one-year-old gunman who wouldn't even look into the camera, Nadine said, "I forgive you." Continuing to speak through her pain and tears: "You took something very precious from me. I will never talk to her again. I will never, ever hold her again. But I forgive you. And have mercy on your soul."[2]

One by one, family member after family member stood at the microphone, looked at the face on the screen, and repeated the words *forgive* and *mercy*. Hate had attempted to drive out the light, but love would not let it be extinguished. A nonbeliever had murdered believers, but he could not kill their belief. And why? Because words are powerful. They can tear someone down to the lowest depths or take someone to the highest heights. This became beautifully clear at Rev. Clementa Pinckney's funeral where, then-President Barack Obama delivered the eulogy. As he neared the end of his forty-minute message, he paused, and after a few moments of silence, he began to sing the words: "Amazing grace, how sweet the sound . . ." It has been identified as one of the most powerful moments of his presidency.[3]

Words of hate led to destroyed lives and broken hearts. Words of life and love breathe hope into a hopeless situation. The right words can open the window and chase out the darkness. Words can hold the power to both life and death. In other words, there is a realm of purpose beyond a dictionary or glossary. This deeper place of meaning is where we now turn our attention.

The Word That Determines All Other Words

There is a Word that has power beyond human comprehension. There is a name that has all authority in heaven and on earth. "The Word became flesh and dwelt among us. We observed his glory, the glory as the one and only Son from the

Father, full of grace and truth" (John 1:14). The Word . . . the only Son from the Father . . . is Jesus Christ. Scholars have described the Word who was the Son and who was God this way: "who is to God what man's word is to himself, the manifestation or expression of himself to those without him."[4] In other words, no pun intended, Jesus is to God what our words are to us. If our words express the matters of our heart, Jesus is the heart of God walking among us.

And what a name he has. We read often in Scripture about incredible things happening "in Jesus' name": evil's authority is rendered helpless, demons are cast out, all kinds of healings are performed, salvation and conversational intimacy with God is made possible . . . all in the name of Jesus. Jesus is God's heart poured out on humanity, so that we can rediscover the very purpose of humanity. After all, the name *Jesus* means "Jehovah (the Lord) is our salvation" and, thus, emphasizes his humanity. While *Christ* is a title meaning "anointed one" and refers to him being the Messiah, the name Jesus Christ helps us see him as *the only 200 percent being ever to exist because he is all man, all God, all one.*

It is quite interesting that John's Gospel calls Jesus Christ the "Word." Volumes upon volumes of books have been written unpacking this section of the Bible using words that require a decoder ring to understand. But in the end, referring to Jesus as the Word speaks to the idea that he is truth, the one true God that has existed from eternity past and will continue to exist for eternity future. He was the truth in the sacred agreements, known as covenants, in the Old Testament. He was the truth of the law. He was the truth that preserved the Jewish people against all odds. He is the truth, the Word, that has always been present. All that we know, say, and believe makes sense in and through the Word, Jesus. Therefore, we say, *Jesus is the Word that determines all other words.*

This is further emphasized when James writes: "no one can tame the tongue. It is a restless evil, full of deadly poison" (James 3:8). At first glance, this seems like an incredibly defeating statement. One might be tempted to think: *Well, I can't do anything about it so why try?* But don't grow weary in your desire to use your words well. You see, the tongue can't be tamed, but it can be transformed. And once it is transformed, along with the rest of us, by the glorious work of the gospel, then it must be kept in check. Remember, God transforms us, and then gives us everything we need to live a transformed life (i.e., the Holy Spirit, the Bible, and the church). As it pertains to our words, it is particularly helpful to remember that "our struggle is not against flesh and blood, but . . . against evil" (Eph. 6:12).

When Paul is describing this very real battle that all Christians fight, he lists five defensive components that he refers to as, "the full armor of God, so that you may be able to resist in the evil day" (v. 13). Because our words have the power to be a "restless evil" (James 3:8), the first piece of armor mentioned is truth (Eph. 6:14). That's right, we are redeemed by the "Word became flesh," and we can use our words in a healthy and effective way because "the word of God is living and effective."[5]

Where Do Words Come From?

Jesus gives us a clear statement concerning the conception of our words, but does so using imagery that would leave a lasting imprint on his audience. He teaches us that "a tree is known by its fruit" (Matt. 12:33). Essentially, good trees produce good fruit and bad trees produce bad fruit. Jesus is comparing the tree to one's heart and the fruit to the words that come out of one's mouth. He calls our hearts either a "storeroom of good" or "storeroom of evil" (v. 35). In either case, "the mouth speaks from the overflow of the heart" (v. 34).

Jesus is the light of the world, and he illuminates the entirety of our existence. It is all important to him. Every pulse, every breath, every heartbeat within our chest matters to God. This is why our words should be an outward expression consistent with an inner reality. Remember the good tree was once a bad tree that God transformed from the roots to the fruits. This is why our words are now sacred. The fourth-century theologian and philosopher Saint Augustine of Hippo explained it this way:

> Let each one then be a good tree; let him not suppose that he can bear good fruit, if he remains a corrupt tree. There will be no good fruit, but from the good tree. Change the heart, and the work will be changed. Root out desire, plant in charity. "For as desire is the root of all evil," so is charity the root of all good.[6]

If charity is the root of all good, then God's love is where all good comes from.

Words then cannot be fully understood when only studied from the neck up. The right kind of words are the overflow of a redeemed heart. Our hearts are literally a storeroom of good. God has given us a warehouse where our words should come from and he calls it "the heart."

When the Bible speaks of the heart, it is referring to the center of our being. Jesus' phrase "the storeroom of good" (Matt. 12: 35) is such an appropriate term because so much activity happens in that storeroom. One scholar summarized it this way:

> The "heart" signifies the total inner self, a person's hidden core of being (1 Pt 3:4), with which one communes, which one "pours out" in prayer, words, and deeds (Ps 62:8; Mt 15:18–19). It is the genuine self, distinguished from appearance, public position, and physical presence (1 Sm 16:7; 2 Cor 5:12; 1 Thes 2:17). And this "heart-self" has its own nature, character, and disposition (Dn 4:16; 7:4).[7]

What Do Words Reveal?

Words reveal the real you.

Socrates once said, "Speak, that I may see thee." The great philosopher wasn't blind. He was merely explaining that when you speak from the overflow of the inner self, the real you will become truly visible. Now some of us may be thinking: *Yeah, but you can fake your words, so people believe you are a "good tree" when actually you're corrupt.* It is true that you can fake it, but that doesn't change the principle that Jesus is teaching. These kinds of words are simply fruit that look good on the outside but, to go back to Jesus' imagery, are actually rotten on the inside. So, the principle is still the same, "for the mouth speaks from the overflow of the heart" (Matt. 12:34).

Our words, wherever they may appear, attest to the inner self. Who you are on the inside will eventually and inevitably be revealed through your communication. Therefore, our words can reveal that we are a person of good or bad character. Throughout all of history this principle has been true. But living in our technologically advanced, experience-is-the-ultimate-goal age, there is a new twist on this timeless truth.

For thousands of years, we've all used words in similar ways. People bargained in the markets; worshiped in their respected churches, synagogues or temples; philosophized; watched plays in the theatre; and debated in the governments. All of this and not to mention the words shared at homes over dinner or around a fire through stories. What is different now has to do with the shelf life of our words. And we can completely thank computerization for that little wrinkle. What we say, follows us for the rest of our lives, and hangs around after we are gone. You can post a picture in college doing something you would never want your kids to see, but one day those little tech-savvy digital natives might find the fraternity version of their father. The internet isn't perfect, but it does have a perfect memory.

We live in a world where people feel empowered to say or do just about anything on social media platforms—from young teens dancing provocatively on TikTok in hopes of earning millions of views, to supposedly mature Christians spouting off at the mouth tweeting like they don't have any sense. Oh, and let's not even mention the individuals who feel the need to share every feeling on social media as if it were their therapist.

Of course, there are great benefits to the access of the age we live in. I follow many people across social media because their content is helpful, edifying, and encouraging, or just plain inspirational. I follow others because they are hilarious. Seriously, who doesn't enjoy a well-thought-out meme? It may be an art form unto itself. Others I follow because it's an extension of our friendship or working relationship.

All I am saying is that social media has ushered in an era where the thoughts we share, the videos we watch, and the stuff we like all go into one big large digital footprint. Maybe we understand it better this way: the entirety of our activity in a digital world, and the experience it creates, all contributes to a story. And each day we interact, the more we add to that story. Like all stories, there is one dominant theme that rises to the surface. So, I guess my question is this: *Does the theme of your social activity communicate you are a good tree that bears healthy fruit?* Words have always revealed, but in a social media age we are revealed in a more public and permanent manner.

How Powerful Are Words?

There is an old adage. One that we actually don't know the precise age or origin. This leaves us, sadly, with no one to blame for the following:

> Sticks and stones may break my bones,
> But words will never hurt me.

Sure, sticks and stones can cause physical damage. Hopefully, that goes without saying. This was a maxim that little kids could use to ward off a bully's insult, so the second line is meant to be the point. I'm sure we all wish it were true. Unfortunately, it isn't as easy as telling someone, "Your words will never harm me!" Because to suggest words lack the power to hurt is completely false. It doesn't matter if you are seven or seventy, words can hurt, and furthermore, can leave an open, lasting wound.

When I was fresh out of college, I served as a youth pastor at a church located along Florida's Panhandle. I was young, idealistic, and completely void of any ministerial experience. Honestly, it was an incredible season of ministry. I felt like I learned more from the students than they did from me. We tried so many things to show the love of Jesus and just be a part of realizing the desires of God for our city. One of our projects was to help students become influencers on their campuses. Naturally, we put a leadership team together. All were welcome to be a part of the leadership team as long as they were willing to work hard and serve well.

Unfortunately, there was one young lady who continued to show up for our leadership team development time but didn't demonstrate a servant's heart. What I mean by that is she worked hard, believing that leadership was all about checking boxes and completing tasks. This was the opposite of what we were seeking. To be fair, part of it was probably my fault, being young and lacking wisdom. You see, the approach to leadership I was trying to teach is that our "work" and "service" is born out of an identity. In other words, we steward our influence for the glory of God because leadership is devotional before it is practical.

After a series of unfortunate meetings where she was quite rude, and after more meetings to encourage her in the right direction, I had to make a tough decision. I shared with her that she had to rise above her own attitude before she would ever have a positive influence on someone else. Then, I asked her to step off the leadership team so we could simply focus on her personal growth. First, she cried, then she got mad, then said a couple of choice words to myself and the female youth worker present, and finally walked out, slamming the door behind her.

That night her dad called me at my apartment. I could barely get "hello" out of my mouth before he began to tear me down, and there was no bleep button for this conversation. Seriously, this guy was a deacon at our church, but he communicated like he was trying to go viral, for all the wrong reasons, before viral was a thing. I don't remember much of what he said as he shared my litany of inadequacies for being a minister. But the twenty-two-year-old version of myself remembered the last words he said before hanging up on me: "You are the worst youth pastor we have ever had!"

Like I said, I was twenty-two when I heard those words. After the call, I sat on my hand-me-down couch in my cheap apartment that I couldn't even afford on the salary I was earning, and thought: *Maybe he is right.* I would struggle with that one little statement for more than ten years. No matter how the Lord blessed or what good things were happening, there was always a little voice in the back of my head saying, *You're the worst.*

I struggled for ten years because words are powerful! Proverbs teaches that "Death and life are in the power of the tongue" (Prov. 18:21). I love the way that Eugene Peterson shares this truth out of James:

> A bit in the mouth of a horse controls the
> whole horse. A small rudder on a huge ship in
> the hands of a skilled captain sets a course in

the face of the strongest winds. A word out of
your mouth may seem of no account, but it can
accomplish nearly anything—or destroy it!

It only takes a spark, remember, to set
off a forest fire. A careless or wrongly placed
word out of your mouth can do that. By our
speech we can ruin the world, turn harmony
to chaos, throw mud on a reputation, send
the whole world up in smoke and go up in
smoke with it, smoke right from the pit of
hell. (James 3:3–6 MSG)

Think about the negative power of words. A wrongly
motivated, poorly spoken word can set someone's world on
fire. The wrong words can leave everything around it in ashes.
And the person with a storeroom of evil leaves a wake of
destruction behind them. A life is truly wasted when its words
are careless. I know this is a strong conclusion, but it is better
not to have lived than to live among the ruins of lives you have
destroyed.

Take heart because wasted words will not write the end of
the story. Let the redeemed speak from the storeroom of good:

- May our words be a blessing to our brothers and sisters (James 3:10).
- Oh that we would speak pleasant words
  that are like a honeycomb (Prov. 16:24).
- Because "knowledgeable lips are a rare
  treasure" (Prov. 20:15).
- Let us be the ones whose words protect
  life (Prov. 13:3).

- And have the gentle answers that turn away anger (Prov. 15:1).
- Ours are words that bring healing (Prov. 15:4), wisdom, and loving instruction (Prov. 31:26).
- "May the words of my mouth and the meditation of my heart be acceptable to you, LORD, my rock and my Redeemer" (Ps. 19:14).

The right words are satisfying to the soul and edifying to others. Just as the wrong words can ruin a life, so the right ones can save a life. In Matthew 12, Jesus is not simply speaking about the manner in which we communicate, but the meaning and substance of what we communicate. It is the combination of compassion with the right content that characterizes those who speak from a "storeroom of good." We leave in our wake lives filled with hope. And let it be understood from the rooftops to the streets down below: a life well lived spends its days emptying the storeroom of good so that others may experience the goodness of God.

A Word on "Cancel Culture"

In the handful of years leading up to the pandemic of 20/21, we saw a rise in national and cultural awareness. Two powerful examples include the #MeToo movement and the national outrage and marches against racial injustice. Somewhere in recent years we have also seen the rise of call out culture which has given birth to something called "cancel culture," usually utilizing the hashtag #cancelled.

> *Cancel culture* refers to the popular practice of withdrawing support for (*cancelling*) public figures and companies after they have done or said something considered objectionable or offensive. *Cancel culture* is generally discussed as being performed on social media in the form of group shaming.[8]

I get it. Public figures or companies do bad or questionable things, and the masses use their influence to voice disgust through shame and disassociation. But can we, for a moment, question whether this is the proper use of a Christian's words? Are we called to shame others, to cancel them into submission?

Cancel culture is not God-honoring for one simple reason: *anything that is shame-based is not Christ-centered*. Those who have been redeemed fully realize this. After all, we should have been cancelled because of our opposition to God. Yet, when we opposed God, he supported us. When we ran from Jesus, he waited for us to come to our senses and then he ran to us. When we were full of sin and shame, he bore our sin and shame so we could be free. When we were wandering in the darkness of our rebellion, he punched holes in the darkness to redeem us. The redeemed should never join the chorus of cancel culture because we are too busy singing "Amazing Grace."

In all my travels, I've had the opportunity to do a few events with the incredible hip-hop artist Kevin Burgess, known as KB. Every time I get the chance to talk to him, I always learn something. He is truly an artist motivated by the goodness of God and seeking to do all things to His Glory Alone (HGA). His perspective on cancel culture is a perfect summary of what we have been discussing:

This is the church.
We will rebuke you when you are wrong.
We will forgive you when you repent.
But we will not cancel you when you are
    down . . . for Christ will not cancel us.
"Cancel culture" is not kingdom culture.
We don't just applaud the righteous, we
    restore the fallen.[9]

The biggest problem with cancel culture is that it doesn't offer hope. And a redemptive outcome is not the goal, though it sometimes happens. We, brothers and sisters, are the most hope-filled people on the planet. Ours is a redemptive story, and we want others to be redeemed as well. So yes, we won't tolerate injustice or abuse, we won't turn a blind eye to corruption, and we will never endorse any activity that marginalizes the vulnerable. We will stand on the frontlines caring for and defending the targets of such abuse. We are pro-accountability. But, you see, we are also a tribe that will not cancel what Christ seeks to redeem.

Words might seem trivial, but we've seen when they are powerful. They are a gift from God and should never be wasted, but rather weighed and stewarded. The "Word became flesh" has indeed granted each of us "grace upon grace from his fullness" (John 1:14, 16). The Word put skin on and lived among us, demonstrating the purposefulness of the overflow from our storerooms of good. Those who follow Jesus are motivated differently. We think and speak as those on a journey to our heavenly home. We live in the beginning place where there isn't any real estate for idols or wasted words. In the beginning place, we know our words are meant to be hopeful and life-giving. We talk as those filled and overflowing with God's goodness. Emily Dickinson wrote:

> A word is dead
> When it is said,
> Some say.
> I say it just
> Begins to live
> That day.

So, go on and let the storeroom overflow with goodness to those around you. Let your words live beyond just the moment they are spoken out loud. And along the way, ask: "LORD, set up a guard for my mouth; keep watch at the door of my lips" (Ps. 141:3).

Rest

Step 4: Discover Your Rest Cycle

Our bodies are designed to rest in the form of sleep each night. Doctors and scientists keep discovering the benefits to a good night's sleep. According to the U.S. Department of Health and Human Services, the right amount of sleep benefits mental and physical health. Additionally, up through our teenage years, it supports growth and development. Did you know that sleep can even help repair the heart and blood vessels?[1] But even though our bodies are designed to rest, human beings are the only mammals on the planet that willingly delay sleep.[2]

Now, let me confess something: I struggle with getting a good night's sleep. In his children's classic *The BFG*, the Welsh novelist Roald Dahl tells the story of how a little girl living in an orphanage forms an unusual friendship with the only kind giant from Giant Country. In the book, the little girl, Sophie, spots a giant late at night during the witching hour, that moment in the night when all the dark things come out from hiding. Because the giant was seen, he must then take her back to Giant Country out of fear that Sophie would tell others of the existence of giants. From there, a friendship is born and adventures galore follow. It is really a beautiful story.

I often find myself struggling in the night for sleep, much like Sophie. And if I allow myself to think for more than a minute or two, then the witching hour becomes my wondering hours. And during my wondering hours I fill journals with thoughts, research ideas I don't fully understand, and study the Scriptures. Often times I'll read for a bit, then wander around outside listening to the sound of the St. John's River filling the night air while I look at the stars and try not to trip. I don't know if it has anything to do with twenty years on the road chasing late-night flights, or if it's just the way I am wired. In any case, the struggle is real.

Doctors have discovered that we sleep in cycles. A cycle of sleep has five phases and usually takes about ninety minutes to complete before starting over. If our goal is to get a healthy eight hours of sleep, then we will go through five sleep cycles.

I believe there is another five-cycle rest, but this one should occur throughout the entirety of a person's journey. Rest is undoubtedly a gift from God. It is also seen all throughout the grand narrative of Scripture. Yet the idea of rest, beyond just sleeping, has largely been lost on our fast-paced society. If you were to ask the average student who is taking a full load of classes, involved in a club or two, goes to church, and has a part-time job about rest . . . then you would probably get the same answer from a mom of two or three kids, armed with her mom purse, a latte, and a minivan. Rest has become a foreign concept in our world. And yet, it has been a shared value for much of the history of the church.

My hope in this chapter is that we will rediscover the purpose of rest, of which I believe there are five primary types identified in the Bible that together create *the rest cycle of the redeemed*.

The Rest Cycle of the Redeemed

A Journey of Rest

There is a rest only available to those who wish to break free from a life of trying too hard. To those who have carried a weight never intended for their shoulders. Those seeking to fit into an impossible template. You show up to as much as you can. You lift up as many as you can through your energy. You walk the halls with a full backpack, drive to the activities with the minivan loaded up, or simply chop away at a task list that never seems to shrink. You volunteer, give, sing, smile, set up, tear down, attend midweek youth group, sign up for the latest Bible study, catch up on podcasts. You rush to be home before home has gone to bed. You care for the home, hoping the home will all come together before the day slips away to slumber.

You so want your home screen to be your real home. There is a deep-seeded desperation for posts that feel like an incantation to become an incarnation. Whether at work, school, home, church, or something else . . . you hope the smiles are believed and showing up is enough.

But in the end, you actually want someone to show up for you. You don't dare utter the words because of some ill-informed view of humanity and weakness. But really, you are the one that needs the energy to be lifted up, to be cared for, and to be listened to. You need some of that energy you are giving away to be directed at your real struggles. You want the weight of always living up to some fictional standard or trying to be someone you're not to be lifted. You want to wake up and realize this was all a dream and that there is actually a better way.

Well, guess what? THERE IS A BETTER WAY! A better way is *exactly* what Jesus teaches. And he invites us to wake up to it when he says, "Come to me, all of you who are weary and burdened, and I will give you rest" (Matt. 11:28). What is the prerequisite for experiencing a rest from the fatigue of simply trying to do life and Christianity well? *Are you weary and burdened?* Are you trying too hard to be the perfect version of what you think you should be? Let me share a secret that few people realize in a socially saturated society: *the perfect story we so desperately seek to project is nothing more than a manufactured myth.*

Let's put it another way. If we claim to follow Jesus and can manage our faith on our own, then it's probably not biblical Christianity. God is not the cosmic cheerleader standing on the sidelines of life, shouting purpose-filled pithy statements and hoping they reach our ears. The image we have in the Scriptures is of God who is both for us, with us, and fighting on our behalf.

He searches for us when we hide in our shame.

He provides refuge so we can have rest from the storm.

He goes through the fire with us.

He provides when we stumble into a wilderness of our own making.

He sits next to us as we weep over the lostness of others.

He chases us down, meeting us on the road to our next bad decision.

He searches the forest to bring us back to the flock.

He illuminates every dark corner because we are cherished.

He stood in the gap between God's wrath and our sin, making a way where there was no way.

All of Scripture shouts in one chorus that God's been with us, working in and through history so that the Messiah could be born to set his people free. Sure, we are broken and messed up beyond repair. That's okay, because God doesn't seek to repair us; he seeks to redeem us. And when he redeems us, he offers himself to us. If you are redeemed, then Jesus is relationally present throughout the entirety of your life, and his presence is sustaining. God's presence is God's provision, plain and simple. We can rest in the journey no matter how difficult it may be because God is with us. We have been given redemption rest because the Redeemer is forever present.

"Weary and burdened" was the language often used when referring to the daily labor of carrying a pack on one's back.[3] A worker who had carried a pack all day was, as my granddad used to say, "dog tired." They needed relief and rest.

Now imagine this: a worker picks up a pack that needs to be delivered to a city in a far-off distant land. It is a trip that will take weeks to accomplish, as he will have to travel over a harsh and dangerous landscape. Now, imagine that he picked up the wrong pack. Through the journey he faced cruel weather conditions, wild animals, and even had to navigate carefully so he wouldn't come in contact with thieves. He endured a journey protecting and caring for something he was never intended to carry.

Some of us are just daily exhausted, down in the depths of our souls. As described earlier, we try and try and try some more. But I wonder if we are carrying around a pack that wasn't meant for us? I wonder if too many of us are shouldering the burden of perfection and, thus, our pack is filled with worry and anxiety. Or maybe something else is in your pack like financial stress, or a strained marriage. There are so many burdens in this broken world, none of which God wants us to shoulder alone. In fact, Jesus invites us to set down our packs filled with burdens and, "Take up my yoke and learn from me, because I am lowly and humble in heart, and you will find rest for your souls. For my yoke is easy and my burden is light" (Matt. 11:29–30).

Let's talk about the word *yoke* for a moment. This was typically a piece of wood that was placed on two or more animals so they could work in harmony together. When they were yoked together under this piece of wood, they acted as one agricultural machine. The yoke was a tool for submission. Now, the Jewish people were used to this word being used as a synonym for submission. For example, they understood "the yoke of the law" to mean submission to the law. Nevertheless, the original meaning of yoke is the piece of wood carved to fit around animals so they may work together.

This is where history gets fun! Where would a farmer purchase a yoke or have a yoke fashioned? A carpenter. And what was Joseph's trade that he had taught Jesus? Carpentry. Jesus would have literally carved many yokes for customers throughout his years in Joseph's workshop. So, Jesus is inviting his listeners to put down their packs and submit to his way and teachings. Now when he says that "my yoke is easy," he isn't suggesting that "if you follow me, you can be lazy and do nothing all day, every day." The word *easy* is a Greek word that means "well-fitting."[4] When someone would have a yoke created for their animals, all kinds of measurements would be taken so that the yoke could be customized to the animals' dimensions. Jesus was saying that each one of us are tailor-made to be in relationship with him. The reason we can find rest in the journey is because we are stepping in the footsteps of Jesus. In his footsteps, living under his authority, we can have confidence and peace. Why? Because then we have discovered life's greatest treasure: the answer to the question: *Where do I belong?*

Jesus was suggesting that we are all created to live in relationship with him. And until we live according to his ways and desires, we will never find rest for the journey. Let's summarize Jesus' invitation to us all: *put down and stop living in submission to the burdens you were never intended to carry, and discover that you were created to follow me—there you belong and there you will find rest.*

A "Jump-Start Your Week" Rest

If we understand what it means to have rest in Jesus, we can turn our attention from redemption rest to a relaxing rest. Each of us on a regular basis needs to take a rest break from the spectacle of activities that consume our time. There is a type of rest in Scripture that would be the modern equivalent of just chilling out. One example occurs in the midst of a particularly busy season of Jesus' ministry. He had sent his twelve disciples out in pairs to minister. By multiplying their efforts, they covered a lot of ground. Even King Herod heard all that was being done in Jesus' name, which contributed to John the Baptist's death. When the Twelve returned to Jesus and shared with him all they had experienced, he sensed a fatigue in them and said, "Come away by yourselves to a remote place and rest for a while" (Mark 6:31).

The twelve disciples were tired . . . they needed rest . . . and Jesus facilitated rest. If you are anything like me, then this type of rest is one of the hardest to accomplish. I wear a lot of hats, just like many of you. I run a nonprofit, maintain a preaching and speaking schedule, author books—Oh and I'm married to the greatest wife on the planet and together we parent six awesome kiddos! Between work, travel, writing, kids' school with all the extracurriculars, and church, I'm doing my best some days to just give my wife a kiss as we pass each other in the hall. But herein is a dangerous lie: *I'm too busy to take time to rest.* This lie has also given birth to the myth that *I'll have time to recharge my batteries later on.* These lies and myths leave us fatigued and barely able to recognize the face staring back in the mirror.

First, let us agree that if the disciples needed rest from their activities, then so do we. And second, if they could make time for rest when the whole world needed to hear the good news of Jesus, then so can we. With that in mind, let us now turn to the practical question of how to create a rhythm of truly relaxing rest.

Relaxation can come in many forms, so let's begin with the end in mind. The purpose of this type of rest is to take a respite from the demands of life so we can fully experience life and meet all of its demands. Working backwards, then, we must discover what gives us a break from the grind of life. The Greek word Jesus used for rest literally means "to make, to cease, to stop or hinder from a thing."[5] Jesus wanted them to stop and take some time to be refreshed and refilled. Jesus knew the importance of rest, and the consequences of not receiving it. Here are a handful of real consequences to our lives if we live without this type of rest:

> If we do not disengage, our engagement will grow increasingly ineffective.

> A lack of rest gives way to self-deception that says, "All of life is up to me."

> When we don't rest, the ones we love the most receive a lesser-than version of us.

> If business becomes the norm, then our souls become numb to the most important stuff.

> When rest is subtracted from our lives, so is our desire/capacity to look at the stars and be captured by the wonder of it all.

> A failure to rest often leads to a restlessness for all the wrong things.

If those are just some of the consequences of not resting, let us now turn our attention to the practical steps to creating a rhythm of relaxation. There are just three simple parts to the process, that when applied, will take us one step closer to the overarching goal of a rest cycle for one's life.

Step 1: Plan and manage your time with rest as a weekly priority. The type of rest that refreshes and affords us the ability to reengage our responsibilities begins with a spirit of intentionality. The reason this type of rest is so hard to accomplish is because it is so easy to ignore or leave unchecked on our to-do lists. Therefore, time management is strategically essential to maintaining the margins needed for rest. Now, here is the beautiful part: you get to choose how you manage your time. There isn't a superior time management system, no matter what is advertised. The ones that work, primarily work because they are adaptable to a person's stage of life and the person works the system. Big calendars that take the long look, daily paper planners that act as a quasi-journal-meets-task management, digital systems with all the customization features, and the list goes on and on. At the end of the day, a plan works when you work the plan. So let's take ownership of our time, and let's prioritize a regular rhythm of retreat, or at some point in the not-too-distant future we may suffer a devastating, exhausting defeat. In short, retreat regularly or take the chance of suffering defeat permanently.

Step 2: Create or go to an environment that is a shift from your daily grind. When Jesus took the Twelve away for some rest, the next verse reads: "And they went away in the boat into a lonely place in private."[6] In other words, Jesus knew that for rest to happen they needed a change of scenery. Now, at first glance, "a lonely place" seems a bit depressing, especially for all the extroverts. So instead of a lonely place, let's call it "the place of a relaxing pace." It's probably helpful for us to have a working definition of this place with a twist for modern-day application. Jesus wanted his disciples to go to a different environment that has a much slower pace. Therefore, "the place of a relaxing pace" is *an environment that offers the ability to temporarily disconnect from the good work we are otherwise involved in, so that we may become refreshed and reenergized.* A lonely place isn't necessarily a place where you are alone, though it could be, but rather a place of enjoyment and relaxation.

In the book of Mark, Jesus took a break from his ministry activities eleven times. Think about that for a moment. There are eleven instances where Jesus changed the agenda, took a break, or simply went to a different environment. When Jesus invites us to follow him, it's not always into the arena of culture to fight the good fight. Sometimes the Good Shepherd invites us to a shady corner just outside the grazing grounds. And there, in the cool of the shade under a tree just off the beaten path, Jesus sits with us. There might be an occasional breeze, possibly some good conversation, or maybe just enjoying the soundtrack of nature. He invites us to rest. The very act of Jesus resting with the Twelve is a personal invitation for us to come to the lonely place—which is really anything but.

Step 3: Select an activity that reenergizes you mentally, physically, and emotionally. We are not clones. Therefore, it would be naive or arrogant, or maybe both, to assume that we will all rest in the same manner. Some people are reenergized by joining a basketball or pickleball league; others read a book by themselves in a coffee shop; some go to the movies; some just go for a long walk. We are all wired so differently that, sometimes, the most productive activity is inactivity. Others are wired so that a different activity is more productive. The sad thing is many of us haven't discovered what it means to get into our metaphoric boats and sail away for an afternoon to a lonely place in private.

Okay, here's the deal: go on a quest for rest. What do you enjoy? What do you need? What have you never tried? What's a skill that you may have but never taken the time to cultivate? Join a team, take a class, get into a book or art club, go to a museum, schedule your husband to take the kids out once a week to the park down the street so you can read for a few minutes and then nap, lock your phone away, or stream your favorite show. You get to decide your lonely place . . . so try and try and keep trying until you discover what offers respite and rest. Choose a type of rest that makes the whole you a better you. BUT CHOOSE! Choose because you want to be a better son or daughter, a better parent or spouse, a better student or employee, a better friend or church member. But most of all, choose because on this little blue marble spinning round and round the sun, the king of the universe has invited you to take a break and sit with him in the shade.

A "Jolly Holiday" Rest

The crowning achievement of Walt Disney's historic movie career came to us in 1964 by way of *Mary Poppins*. It is an amazing film that combines all the movie magic techniques learned over forty years, going all the way back to the early 1920s with the short-film cartoons Disney produced for a local movie theater. *Mary Poppins* was the only film Disney created that earned a Best Picture nomination at the Oscars. One of my favorite moments in the film is when Mary Poppins, the two children she cares for, and Burt—who happens to be a jack-of-all-trades—go on a jolly holiday. This is accomplished through magic when the four of them jump through a chalk drawing Burt had created on a local sidewalk outside of the park. Once inside the painting, adventures included horse racing, playing at a fair, saving a fox from its would-be hunters, and teatime served by an amazing quartet of penguin waiters. The penguins help with the singing of the incredible song "Jolly Holiday," while dancing with Burt. (Fun sidenote: Some of the profits from *Mary Poppins* helped build the monorail system at Walt Disney World.)

It doesn't require magic to get away for an extended period of time for rest. Often times in the United States, we call this an annual vacation. Much of Europe simply refers to it as "going on holiday." In either case, a break from school or work by vacating your normal life is a form of rest that is important.

And lest we think getting away annually for rest is a modern-day invention, the Jewish observed at least three festivals a year:

> "Celebrate a festival in my honor three times a year. Observe the *Festival of Unleavened Bread*. As I commanded you, you are to eat unleavened bread for seven days at the appointed time in the month of Abib, because you came out of Egypt in that month. No one is to appear before me empty-handed. Also observe the *Festival of Harvest* with the firstfruits of your produce from what you sow in the field, and observe the *Festival of Ingathering* at the end of the year, when you gather your produce from the field." (Exod. 23:14–16, emphasis added)

These festivals were all meant to signify an important event or time of year in the Jewish calendar. The Festival of Unleavened Bread, also called Passover, commemorated the hardships endured and the ultimate deliverance from Egyptian bondage. The Festival of Harvest, also known as Pentecost or the Feast of Weeks, was purposed to dedicate the firstfruits of the wheat harvest. The Festival of Ingathering, also known as the Feast of Tabernacles, was designed to celebrate the completion of the harvest.[7]

While each festival had a specific role of honor and dedication, the pilgrimage and ensuing celebration was a blessing nonetheless in the midst of this life of labor and toil.[8] The people looked forward to the festivals. It was something that allowed them to vacate their normal workweeks and be a part of something special.

As Christians, we don't have festivals in the same manner as the Jewish people in the Old Testament. But I do think there is something to be learned from their trifecta of gatherings and all the rest they offered. A rhythm of annual rest can be a healthy practice. And, much like relaxing rest, it requires a spirit of intentionality and a place to rest and have fun with loved ones.

I grew up in a typical middle-class family. By "typical" I mean we lived well but were by no means going on upper-class type vacations. A little condominium or hotel, maybe in the off-season when it was more affordable, and a beach nearby was all we needed. You can't buy the sense of wonder when a little kid sees the ocean for the first time in a year out of the back seat of a station wagon. We played every day until we were too sunburned or exhausted to jump in the waves or build one more sandcastle. I remember my mom taking us on night hikes along the beach to look for crabs and enjoy the night air. I also remember, on more than one occasion, having to take a day and go play putt-putt golf or see a movie because our pasty skin needed a break from the sun. My dad played and fished with us every day, my mom hiked with us and allowed us to eat sugary cereal (you know the kind other kids brag about eating) every day.

We were just happy being together. Making good memories doesn't require a certain socioeconomic standing in society. I'm pretty sure the main ingredients are time, love, imagination, and fun. My parents always stressed to us that our annual vacation to the beach was a blessing, because all good things come from God. We grew up believing that God was happy when we went on vacation. We believed he was smiling as he watched us jump into wave after wave, and maybe even chuckled when we ordered an ice cream that was way too big to eat before it melted, making our hands sticky.

My parents did vacation right, and it really wasn't about how much money they could or could not spend. Maybe that's why I have continued that same tradition with my own kids. When they jump off my shoulders in the pool, or when my five-year-old picks up a seashell in the midst of thousands of seashells and declares it a treasure, or when we are walking the beaches after dark hoping to find something cool . . . I believe God is happy. God delights when friends and family, after honoring him through their responsibilities, go away and have fun together. After all, what father doesn't enjoy watching his kids build sandcastles?

A "Join with Community" Rest

The pandemic caused us to rethink so many aspects of our lives. Who would have thought that our digital age would have an early onset of "screen fatigue"? And the term *essentially* took on a whole new meaning, along with the debate concerning what is and is not essential. One of the things I missed the most during months of quarantine and no in-person gatherings was the rhythm of congregating with other people who love Jesus. Nothing compares to the experience of a space being filled with one collective voice in song, listening to the Bible taught, celebrating with one another, serving each other, and just being together. One of the beautiful aspects about being redeemed is getting around others who have been redeemed. It strengthens our faith and deepens our gratitude.

Church is essential.

Whether you are an introvert or extrovert, Enneagram 5 or 7, your personality type is some animal combination, or just a couple of letters . . . we all need each other. We were created for relationship, and because God has given us life, a community of the redeemed gathering just makes God-honoring sense. Now, let's be honest about something: it was never ideal to gather with others looking back at you on a glowing screen. But the medium by which the church is expressed does not devalue its necessity to our lives. The apostle Paul taught us to "[bear] with one another" (Col. 3:13) in his letter to the Colossian believers. That means that being a part of a church community won't always be easy, but it is forever worth it.

The church is the fellowship of the redeemed. The book of Hebrews teaches us the greatest way we can encourage each other is through "not neglecting to gather together" (Heb. 10:25). Because when we gather, we are able to "consider one another in order to provoke love and good works" (v. 24). To show how important this has been throughout the history of church gatherings, we now turn to John Chrysostom, a church father who died in AD 407 and had a tremendous impact on the early church:

> "And let us consider one another," he says, "to provoke unto love and to good works." He knew that this also arises from "gathering together." For as "iron sharpeneth iron" (Prov. 17:17), so also association increases love. For if a stone rubbed against a stone sends forth fire, how much more soul mingled with soul! But not unto emulation (he says) but "unto the sharpening of love." What is "unto the sharpening of love"? Unto the loving and being loved more. "And of good works"; that so they might acquire zeal.[9]

I love the phrase "association increases love." The church is at its best impacting the world when fellowship among its saints is considered an essential priority.

So you might be asking: *What does this have to do with rest?* Remember that rest is something that replenishes the soul. Rest accomplishes something in us that affords us the ability to live and love better. If our association increases love, then fellowship among the saints accomplishes two things by way of rest.

First, it builds us up to walk in the redemption rest because, brothers and sisters, "we have boldness to enter the sanctuary through the blood of Jesus" (Heb. 10:19). Togetherness pleases God and helps us become even more obedient: "Therefore, a

Sabbath rest remains for God's people. . . . Let us, then, make every effort to enter that rest, so that no one will fall into the same pattern of disobedience" (Heb. 4:9, 11). When the redeemed gather, we answer a prayer of Jesus: "I am no longer in the world, but they are in the world, and I am coming to you. Holy Father, protect them by your name that you have given me, so that they may be one as we are one" (John 17:11).

Second, when we gather together regularly to celebrate redemption rest, it is a foreshadowing of the promised future rest in heaven. And that leads us to the final part of the rest cycle of the redeemed.

A "Journey's End" Rest

In heaven's dictionary, it does not contain the words *fatigue* or *tired* or any of the like. If life is a pilgrimage, a journey in which we wander toward our heavenly home, then our future residence is a place of rest. Now we are weary from life's journey, but in heaven we will never tire again. You see, for the Christian, rest is a present reality that hints about our future home. Heaven is restful because heaven is home. In a previous book, I evaluated Paul's life through the lens of pilgrimage and what it would be like to go to heaven: "There were no more moments to experience on this side of the journey. The pilgrimage had come to an end, but a greater story was just beginning. Paul had finished . . . Paul would now begin. And therein lies the glorious outcome for all pilgrims wandering their way homeward—when we finish, it's really just the beginning."[10] If the journey is to the heaven country, then heaven is a place of rest. When we finish, we rest in the greater story that will be experienced, not as citizens from afar, but as residents in the land of our God and people.

There is also a sense that our life's work is completed once we arrive in heaven. I know it's not popular to speak of dying, but death is inevitable. It's amazing how dramatic events seem to simplify what great minds spend generation after generation contemplating. The truth is that you can only die one of two ways: either with or without the Lord. Let's focus on the former. As the apostle John wrote: "Blessed are the dead who die in the Lord . . ." (Rev. 14:13). The word *blessed* is specifically used to remind us of the Beatitudes. The word *beatitude* simply refers to a state of blessedness or happiness. The apostle John is pronouncing a heavenly verdict: *to die in Jesus is to die happy and blessed.*

And what do those who die happy in Jesus receive? "They will rest from their labors, since their works follow them" (Rev. 14:13). In heaven, we are revived and refreshed forevermore. Our labors are over, but our works will follow us to the heaven country. It would seem that the lives we live follow us to the heavenly places. The work we do in this life will serve as a witness in heaven. Let's be incredibly clear: all of the energy and effort of this life is not wasted; it is recognized and rewarded in heaven. The wear and tear on your existence in this life reverberates throughout eternity. We are given the privilege to be counted as faithful and courageous before the throne of God. If heaven's dictionary doesn't have certain words, then we can stand before God and say the dictionary of our pilgrimage didn't contain the words *compromise* or *quit*. Taking the long look is the only way to a blessed rest that lasts forever.

On March 20, 1991, the great musician Eric Clapton was in a nearby hotel getting ready to pick up Conor, his four-year-old son, from a nearby apartment. It was going to be a great father-son afternoon with lunch and a trip to the Central Park

Zoo. As Clapton was preparing for the outing, he received a phone call from his girlfriend, Italian actress Lory Del Santo, crying and screaming hysterically into the phone that Conor was dead. A member of the cleaning crew had left a window to their 53rd story apartment open, and Conor had climbed through and fallen to his death. Clapton described the scene to a British journalist, Sue Lawley, in 1992:

> Clapton says he "went cold" and "shut down right away" after hearing the news. In a state of disbelief, the "Layla" singer remembers rushing from his hotel to the apartment block where he "saw ambulances and fire engines and paramedic vehicles" outside. Upon entering the apartment, then filled with emergency service responders, Clapton recalls feeling like the scene had nothing to do with him. "I felt like I had walked into someone else's life," Clapton told Lawley in measured tones. "And I still feel like that."[11]

In his pain, Clapton turned to his art to mourn and express his grief. There in the quiet recesses of lamenting, one of the greatest musicians the world has ever known wrote two songs about Conor. One was "Circus Left Town," capturing the memory of taking his son to the circus the night before his death. The other was "Tears in Heaven," which would become one of the most well-recognized and personal songs of an illustrious career.

"Tears in Heaven" is a heart-wrenching picture of a father wondering about his son in heaven. Some of the questions Clapton asks in the song are: "Would you know my name?"

"Would it be the same?" "Would you hold my hand?" While much of the song is pain expressed, there are a couple of lines that allow hope to peek through the pain: "Beyond the door, there is peace I'm sure. And I know there will be no more tears in heaven."[12]

A parent should never bury a child. It has to be one of the cruelest things that can happen living in a broken world. Clapton seems to have believed when he wrote the song, if there is a heaven, tears won't be in it. Again, the apostle John is helpful here when he describes heaven this way: "He will wipe away every tear from their eyes. Death will be no more; grief, crying, and pain will be no more, because the previous things have passed away" (Rev. 21:4).

> No one hurts in heaven.

> There we receive rest from the loss and pain of this world.

> In heaven everything makes sense—forever makes sense.

> Heaven is a dream realized that will never be unrealized.

> In heaven there are no doctor appointments or chemo treatments.

> There no one limps, and no one loses.

> In heaven there is only life, and death is a like a redeemed memory from another lifetime.

The rest cycle of the redeemed begins with redemption rest and ends with blessed heaven's rest. Without a spirit of intentionality, rest won't become a reality. I have been apart of cultures that prided themselves on a work ethic that was borderline insanity. Then I have been a part of other cultures that masked laziness as a form of spirituality. Neither approach is God-honoring and both should be taken to the curb to be picked up with the other trash. Rest is not only possible; it is a form of obedience. And if rest is obedience, then to neglect the rest cycle of the redeemed is disobedience. So if you are tired of being tired, fatigued, and so exhausted you can barely remember your name . . . if you are tired of enduring rather than enjoying the moments of life . . . and if you are worn out feeling like you are not the best you . . . then take heart, because the God of the universe is inviting you to rest.

5

Relationships

Step 5: Practice the Art of Relating Well

There are few true originals in this world. We all have the
potential to be one in creation but seem to strive for the car-
bon copy of another's identity. In other words, most of us,
while pretending to be our own person, are really insecure and
just hoping no one figures us out. At least, that is the way I
have felt many times in my own life. To that end, I introduce
Catbird. When I met Catbird, she was in her mid-seventies
and working at the local Western Sizzlin. I met her in such an
establishment because I had recently secured a job in the food
industry as well. If you've never heard of a "Western Sizzlin,"
well then, let me enlighten you. It is simply a local feeding
trough where someone can come and order a buffet filled with
every imaginable greasy comfort food or get something from
the kitchen. The steaks were actually pretty good!

Anyway, back to Catbird. Her job was to maintain the
salad bar and keep it stocked with all the fixings. It was a
large and spacious smorgasbord kind of salad bar, the kind

that seemed to be heavy on everything but salad. In any case, the seemingly endless options of dressings, toppings, iceberg lettuce, and some sort of green pea concoction that erred on the side of mystery made up the vocation of the fascinatingly unique Catbird. To say she was proud of her job would undoubtedly be stretching things a bit. To say she tolerated her job with some measure of disdain would be a more appropriate depiction.

Before I go any further, I never learned her real name. To all who interacted with her, she was simply referred to as Catbird. I am sure she had to have another name. I mean I can't imagine her birth parents named their little girl C-a-t-b-i-r-d. To this day, I can honestly say that I have never met a person more unimpressed by people . . . or their opinions. Catbird was honest to the core, the type of honesty that gets people sued nowadays. If she thought it, then she shared it. And if you didn't like it, the edited version of what she would say is, "Get over it."

This leads me to her unique talent for creatively cursing. By that, I mean she could string words together that, with any other person, would never end up in the same sentence. Cursing came so naturally to her that if one wanted to learn how to curse in style, Catbird could have taught a master class. Sometimes I found myself counting the four-letter words she would express in one sentence and end up missing what she was trying to tell me. This, of course, frustrated her, and then she would direct some colorful vernacular my way that would make a sailor blush. If cursing was an art form, then Catbird was the "Picasso of Profanity."

For some crazy reason, I found myself drawn to her. I would take my breaks at the same time she would, pulling up a chair to eat my lunch or dinner and listen to her wax elegantly about topics that had very little importance in the greater scheme of society. Soon, this twenty-year-old college student waiting tables began cracking jokes with this mysterious lady in her seventies. She rarely shared anything about her life. On the rare occasion I asked something personal, she chuckled at me, letting me know it wasn't any of my business. Then, we would laugh, and the conversation would go another direction.

I could tell that underneath a grocery cart full of opinions, her firm scowl, and foul language that made most people afraid of her was an elderly lady who was very lonely. So at the local feeding trough in a town that you would miss if you blinked, two people found each other and a fantastic friendship began. She was lonely, but the truth is that so was I. I never really seemed to fit in anywhere, so my daily conversations with Catbird became somewhat of a highlight for me. We mostly talked about traveling. She had never really been anywhere outside of east Tennessee and so, with each break, we would discuss a new place I would take her after I graduated. Sitting in the back of the Sizzlin, breathing in enough secondhand smoke to choke a horse, we pretended about the future.

One of my favorite memories of Catbird, which happened more than once, was when a customer would dare complain to her about the salad bar. Or, for example, if she observed someone piling all the imitation crabmeat salad on their plate after just being refreshed. She just didn't care or hesitate. That's right, Picasso would just look that person up and down and then "paint" away. God bless the manager who had to then field complaints about an elderly lady cussing at customers.

When it would happen, I would laugh to myself. Seriously, the audacity of Catbird to commentate on someone working their way through her salad bar! They should have made a reality show out of it.

Sometimes, I would intervene, if for no other reason than I didn't want my friend to get fired. Really, how many times can you insult customers and get away with it? To intervene, I would simply take a blank sheet of paper and write on it, "Catbird the Great." I would tape it to one of the chairs in the restaurant. Then I would go find Catbird painting away and interrupt her by saying, "Ma'am, we have a chair for you right this way." It would confuse both her and the customer she was insulting. She would follow me to the chair and see her sign and begin laughing so loud the entire back side of the restaurant could hear it.

On my last day at the Sizzlin, before graduating from college, I was sad to learn that Catbird wasn't working. After my shift, I went to the manager's office, called the old girl, and said our goodbyes. She cried and honestly, so did I, but I assured her we would see each other again and take that cross-country trip of which we had always talked. I tried one more time and dropped by the restaurant, but she wasn't working then either. It was probably for the best. Catbird didn't care much for sentiment.

Over the years I have often thought about my friend. She was the best—an older woman living in a remote region of Tennessee where small little cities seemed to disappear into the mountains' beautiful landscape. These mountains reminded me of a calm ocean that would rise up and down with the waves, that danced with color during certain times of the year and shined with snow during others. These mountains seemed to say, no matter the weather . . . the warmth or the cold . . . the wind or the rain . . . we are still here, steady through it all. The mountains never change, they never move, and all of life just revolves around or on them. They are steady, unmoving, and yet beautiful, just like Catbird the Great.

The world needs a few more and a few less Catbirds. By that, I mean we don't need more people shouting and cussing and putting people in their place. I think the quota is full of overopinionated individuals who have become inflated with their egocentric agendas. But we do need a few more originals. We need people who will unashamedly be themselves. Don't you think the world would be better off with people who were steadfast in friendship? Don't you think we need the kind of person who shows up when they say they will show up? Don't we need the people who are comfortable in their skin and committed to important things, like the relationships in their lives?

Meanwhile, if you are ever passing through a little town just north of Chattanooga, Tennessee, before the land begins to rise and fall again, stop by the local Western Sizzlin. But if you dare to visit the salad bar, know that you were warned. Oh, and when the Picasso of Profanity is done with you, tell Catbird her old friend says hello.

Relationships are all about relating to another human being in a healthy and positive manner. Catbird taught me, in her unique way, the nature of a genuine and authentic friendship. She was in her mid-seventies, worn and beaten down by life, and I didn't even know her real name . . . yet her friendship filled a void in my life. And in turn, I think our friendship filled a void in her life as well. Now, think about all the potential relationships we could and probably will have in our lives: sibling, parent, spouse, family member, friend, coworker, girlfriend, boyfriend, teammate, employee, employer, student, teacher, and on and on. Instead of just focusing on certain types of relationships, let's look at the tried-and-true way of relating well across the entire landscape of our lives.

To accomplish this, we must begin by asking the right questions. We often look for answers to questions that were never asked or should have never been asked. But for our purposes, the questions are designed to take us on a brief journey, beginning with the origins of relationships and ending with the practical steps we can take in the here and now.

What Is the Original Purpose of a Relationship?

Have you ever read something so many times and yet somehow missed an idea that was right in front of you all along? It's like that time I walked around the house looking for my car keys for thirty minutes, only to have my nine-year-old say, "Daddy, aren't you holding them in your hand?" Okay, confession time. I've looked at the creation narrative (Gen. 1–3) so many times that I spent the better part of my life overlooking one apparent reality: *God addresses aloneness before he ever confronts sinfulness.* We are told that after so much was created, God observed his creation and said, "It is not good for the man to be alone. I will make a helper corresponding to him" (Gen. 2:18).

It is essential for our conversation to know and believe that we were created to be in relationships. Of course, in the creation narrative, the first relationship is the first marriage between husband and wife. Nonetheless, relationships and the ability to relate well are prevalent in the beginning. We see positive and negative examples of relating well. A positive example is that Adam and Eve would obey God and have children. A negative example is that one of their children would murder another.

Being created as relational beings means that to be fully human and lead a life pleasing to God, I must care about relating to others. Let's just get this out of the way for all the introverts, of which I am one: you can't do relationships in a vacuum. Relationships are a responsibility and blessing that must be cared for with a sacred sense of intentionality. After all, any relationship worth having is a relationship worth honoring.

What Role Do Relationships Fulfill in the Life of a Christ-Follower?

Maybe we are better to understand that relationships must show honor at all times. We can't look like Jesus if we aren't willing to honor the various relationships in life's journey. We are taught to "honor everyone. Love the brothers and sisters. Fear God. Honor the emperor" (1 Pet. 2:17). Yes, that pretty much about covers any type of relationship we could have; honor non-Christians, Christians, and those in the government. If there is any confusion, honor *EVERYONE*.

What is meant by the word *honor*, and how do we do it? First of all, an entire book could be written on the subject, tracing "honor" throughout the Bible. Yet, in any case of honor, you will find the sentiment of attributing esteem, worth, dignity, respect, and recognition. It is the respect shown with our hearts, words, and actions. In other words, it is to esteem in thought, word, and deed.[1] To show honor is an act of love.

How much different would our world look if, at the end of the day, we were all known for honoring one another? To honor someone puts me in proximity of their journey. While we can respect people from a distance, showing honor will require a nearness at some point. When this happens, I begin to see that person, and maybe their context, in a whole new light. The decision to honor keeps us humble and guards our minds and hearts against pride. Likewise, esteeming others protects us from being overopinionated. Yes, what a different world it would be indeed. Less noise. More understanding. Less division. More togetherness. Less closed doors. More open hearts to the gospel.

Relationships fulfill a multiplicity of roles in our lives, but each one must begin with the decision to honor. Of course, honor comes easily when we have decided to "above all, put on love" (Col. 3:14). When one discovers that they are clothed in the love of Jesus, then honor becomes a logical posture in life.

In the Greek language, there were often images or word pictures associated with terms. By themselves, some words would conjure up a narrative in the listener's mind, which would then illuminate that person to the meaning of what was said. This is the case with the word *love*. There are four primary words for love in the Greek language. And when we look at them, we see categories for all the different kinds of relationships we will have in our lives.

Storge: "Affectionate for Family" Kind of Love

For so many people, the year 2020 felt like a nightmare, wrapped in a Gothic riddle, during a zombie apocalypse. It was a challenging year, to be sure. No one emerges from a year like that without the scars to prove it. And yet, in some beautiful twist of fate that was the plan all along, it turned out to be the greatest year ever for me and my family. Yet knowing how many people struggled immensely and lost loved ones causes guilt to well up within me even as I write that.

Let me explain. Around ten years ago, my wife and I had three amazing children . . . but we sensed God wasn't done adding to our family. We began to walk down the road of adoption with one child in mind. We went through all the necessary steps to become eligible to have a child placed in our home. It was a frustrating time because every door seemed to get shut in our face.

Furthermore, once we had completed all the legal steps, we had access to a registry that showed all the kids who needed homes. Without going into much detail to avoid throwing shade, we remained stuck. It's like we had purchased a vehicle that we couldn't get to start. Heck, we couldn't even get the engine to turn over in the form of a returned phone call.

During that time, I wrote a book titled *Reimagine* and dedicated it to "the children not yet in our home but already in our hearts. We are imagining a day when our family will be complete."[2] This went on for three to four years and finally we came to believe God wanted us to simply redeem all of this for something else. I was actually embarrassed by that book dedication. I felt like I looked like an idiot who just maybe had good intentions by writing that. We moved on, but not really.

During that time, there was an incredible, young single mom with three amazing kids of her own. She grew up in poverty surrounded by limitations. One day, she sat down and decided to write personal goals for when she would turn thirty years old. They included things like getting an education and a good job. But at the top of the list was to get her children

out of the projects and into an environment with more possibility. Her mother and grandmother had died at a young age
of breast cancer and, sadly, this young mom would encounter
the same fate.

The last three years of her life were a blur of hospital visits
and giving her children every ounce of strength that she could
muster to show them, "Momma loves you!" She died just as
the pandemic became a realization in the United States. Her
last wish was for her three children to remain together and
somehow find a family. By this time, a beautiful and unlikely
cast of characters had come around her. Promises were made
before her last breath was taken.

On an evening in May 2020, my life changed forever. I
was outside walking around the pond in our front yard, just
walking and thinking, primarily about how I would lead our
organization through a pandemic. By that time, I had an idea
and was working it hard . . . but time would tell if it would
work and allow our little nonprofit to keep changing the
world. From a distance, I heard the front door to our home
open and saw my wife, Christina, walking toward me with her
phone in hand. Standing out by the pond, she said, "Stephanie
emailed me. Read this. I have an idea." Stephanie is our friend,
who is a lawyer focusing on child advocacy.

Looking at the screen, I read about three amazing children
whose mother had recently passed away. I looked up from
the email at my wife, smiled, and simply said, "So, what's
your idea?" We held hands and went for a walk that included
prayers, tears, and laughter. Our hearts were strangely warmed,
and we came back to the house and gave Stephanie a call. That
very next weekend, we met Za'Riah, Zi'Yon, and Aryanna for

the first time face-to-face. Within a month, they were in our home.

As I write this, I occasionally look up from this glowing screen to see the pond out front. Gabriel, my fourteen-year-old, and Zi'Yon, my seven-year-old, are fishing. Zi'Yon just caught a small bass, and Gabriel took it off the hook for him and celebrated. They just high-fived, and Gabe is putting fresh bait on Zi'Yon's hook. Three daughters are cuddled on the couch inside the house watching some animated show that involves a horse, and my fourth daughter is in the kitchen with Christina cooking dinner.

When we first brought all the kids together, we essentially doubled our family's size in one moment. Some days, there are challenges; other days, there are more challenges. But every day, there is family affection and love. I don't have an exact date of when it happened, but somewhere in the last year, we became a family. We all just loved and loved and loved each other until loving each other became natural. A lot has happened around that little pond.

Family love is something we choose to bestow on those we see as, well, family. Each night before my kids fall asleep, I tell them I love them "as high as the sky, as deep as the ocean, and all the way to the moon and back." This same love could be applied to other relatives or nonrelatives that become family over time. This is the type of love that is the bedrock of society. It is the glue that holds families together and makes new families feel natural. What is magnificent about this type of love is that it can expand our capacity to love and understand over time. The more we love, the better we become at it, and the more we appreciate those we love. As one author puts it, "affection enlarges our horizons."[3]

Philia: "Friendship Is a Virtue" Kind of Love

The age in which we live has redefined so many English words that have long meant something altogether different. Words like *friend* and *like* and *community* are now based on algorithms configured by someone who understands the matrix-like world where we now find ourselves. And yet, for all that the social age offers, the need for authentic relationships and friendships has never been more crucial . . . which brings us to the second Greek word for love having to do with friendship.

Friendship is so crucial that Aristotle listed it as one of the twelve virtues of a well-lived life. These statements give a sampling of the benefit and purpose concerning the love expressed between friends:

1. "Wishing to be friends is quick work, but friendship is a slow-ripening fruit."
2. "To love someone is to identify with them."
3. "Friendship is essentially a partnership."
4. "My best friend is the man who, in wishing me well, wishes it for my sake."
5. "The antidote for fifty enemies is one friend."

Though Aristotle wrote extensively on friendship, this handful of statements show different characteristics of authentic friendship. The first shows us that true friendship can be wanted now but can only be accomplished over time. The second demonstrates that proximity is essential to loving a friend. Number three states that friendship is a relationship in which all persons are equally invested. Fourth, real friends aren't jealous of the other's success, fortune, or opportunities.

Finally, the love of one friend is more powerful than all of the disparaging efforts of one enemy.

The love between friends is a virtue, and one worth pursuing. Long before I had ever read Aristotle, I had learned many of these qualities from Catbird. Her cigarette ashtrays were filled and emptied many a time before our friendship enjoyed any depth. And the proximity we enjoyed on our breaks or while spending hours wrapping silverware with paper napkins provided an identity. In a way that appeared harsh and downright rude to so many, she actually treated me with kindness and equality. We each wanted what was best for each other. And Catbird was an ally more valuable than I could have ever hoped for.

When studying the Bible, I believe there are four characteristics of friendship that seem to rise to the surface time and again:

- Friends prioritize presence over productivity.
- Friends don't have to qualify to receive quality.
- Friends seek to understand before being understood.
- Friends are quick to set aside self in order to sacrifice.[4]

It could be said that our culture devalues these types of friendships, those that require effort and sacrifice and are free from the entanglement of jealousy and competition. And because the love of friendship is no longer seen as a virtue, even fewer people experience it. After all, as C. S. Lewis writes: "it is the least biological of all our loves."[5] But when love between friends exists, and I can attest to this from experience, it nourishes the soul in a way no other love can.

Eros: "I Am My Love's and My Love Is Mine" Kind of Love

I met Christina by chance—you know the kind. It was a meeting by happenstance that was supposed to happen. It was accidentally on purpose . . . and it changed me forever. Why she gave me the time of day, I will never know. How I mustered the courage to ask her to coffee is a mystery. And what possessed me to reach for her hand on our first date, pull her close, and begin to sing a song as we danced baffles me even now. We danced all those years ago, and we are still dancing today. As we approached our eighteenth wedding anniversary, I put pen to paper and wrote her this poem:

> There was once a man wandering toward a
>   call
> Stumbling scene after scene trying not to fall
> Somewhat rough around the edges, a little
>   tattered
> Kind of raw and scruffy, but none of that
>   mattered
>
> For there was once a woman, with so much
>   purpose to glean
> Dancing seamlessly, flawlessly, scene after
>   scene
> Seeking, venturing, risking, there was so
>   much to attain
> Then came a storm that brought winds of
>   pain

The storm left her battered . . . and that
mattered

Then one day, against all odds, tattered met
battered, and the unexpected took place
On that day, they found themselves, now
wrapped together, in amazing grace
Immediate love gave way to happiness and
bliss
A new journey had begun and not a moment
they would miss

As years passed by the love grew stronger still
Inseparable as they held hands in God's will
Adventures so grand they could hardly
understand the thing
Named Gabe, Charis, Za'Riah, Zi'Yon,
Aryanna, and Mercy who sings

Animals galore from all over the earth
More laughter and memories than any house
could be worth
Silliness and stories, movies and treats
Themed out parties with so many things to
eat

And the story so goes . . .
Tattered and battered fell in love
A love given by the Father above
A home they did build full of gratitude in
heart
A family they did make redeeming every part

A story they continue with no end in sight
A path made straight by the Savior's might

So on any given night, be it week day or end
Down a dirt road and just past the bend
Are the happiest two you will ever see
Usually holding hands, and always will be

There is a love that is reserved for husband and wife. It is a love that characterizes two becoming one. This Greek word for love has two primary characteristics. First, there is a physical attraction between the two future lovers. They see and desire each other. That is to say, they fall in love. Second, this is a love that desires to possess.[6] For example, I would never share my wife with another man. The very idea seems preposterous and unnatural.

The Old Testament King Solomon, whose father was David and mother was Bathsheba, wrote an entire book of the Bible to describe the emotions, beauty, and romance of this type of love. My favorite line in Song of Songs is: "I am my love's and my love is mine" (6:3). The two characteristics of this type of love are present in this short but powerful statement. He obviously desires his lover, and the two are committed to each other; the love they share is not to be shared with anyone else. I know how Solomon feels. When I met Christina, to quote Justin Bieber, I was "running to the altar like a track star."[7]

Agape: "Unconditional Love Reflects the Heart of God" Kind of Love

Rarely in history do so brilliant a mind and so courageous a social justice warrior exist in one person. Such was the case with Dietrich Bonhoeffer. This fascinating figure lived from 1906–1945 and was known for standing against Hitler and Nazism, and subsequently against the Holocaust. He did so during a time when doing such would cost a man his life. As a theologian, he spent a short time as a pastor and most of his time as a professor. Bonhoeffer was one of the few church leaders who stood against the führer and his policies. During his life, he led an association of churches called The Confessing Church, a free Protestant church not controlled by the Nazis. Eventually, the Nazis shut down the seminaries and began imprisoning much of its leadership. Bonhoeffer was involved in a failed conspiracy to assassinate Hitler and overthrow the Third Reich. He was imprisoned in 1943 and executed by hanging in a concentration camp in 1945, only a short time before Hitler committed suicide.[8] Bonhoeffer was just thirty-nine years old at the time of his execution. Scholar. Professor. Church planter. Pastor. Author. Activist. Spy. Assassin. Martyr.

Bonhoeffer lived at a time when the world seemed to be on fire. He lived a short life, but the life he lived was never dormant. And in the midst of all his activities, most of which were illegal under the Third Reich, he relentlessly produced content. At present, there are sixteen volumes of material that have been translated from German to English, which brings us to the fourth Greek word for love. This is God's kind of love, or as Bonhoeffer calls it, "Christian love." During the unprecedented times in which he lived, with the world becoming more uncertain every day, he explained God's kind of love to us.[9]

1. *Christian love is not a human possibility.* In other words, you can't have Christian love divorced from Christ.

2. *It is possible only through faith in Christ and through the work of the Holy Spirit.* It is based on obedience to the word of Christ, who, in meeting our claims, demands that we should give up all claims whatsoever on God or our neighbor. . . . Only through faith in Christ do we understand our love to be the love of God given to our hearts by the Holy Spirit, and our will as conquered by God and obedient to God's will for our neighbor.

3. *Love, as a volitional act, is purposeful.* It is not unfounded affection, but, though possessing the capacity to relinquish all claims, it is a matter of rational reflection as well as human empathy. The purpose of love is exclusively determined by God's will for the other person, namely, to subject the other to God's rule. We must dedicate ourselves entirely and with all our strength to become a means to this end.

4. *It loves the real neighbor.* The person who loves God must, by God's will, really love the neighbor.

5. *That Christian love knows no limits.* It seeks to realize God's rule in each and every place. It only has its limitations where God has set them.

Wow, that's a lot to comprehend! If anything, we can probably all agree, "that Bonhoeffer guy was wicked smart!" But let's see if we can break it down just a bit more. God's love, Christian love, is something made possible in those who follow Jesus. Furthermore, they seek to be obedient and, thus, aren't relying on feelings to love those in proximity (i.e., "neighbor"). This love is an act of obedience to God's desired will, as revealed in the Scriptures. Therefore, Christian love can take a person to the ends of the earth and back, to the darkest corners of society, and to the despised and forgotten. In this sense, God's love is unconditional.

Christian love seeks to answer one question only: *God, where do you want me to go, and who do you want me to love?*

Agape is the fourth and most prominent word used for love in the New Testament. It is the kind of love to which every Jesus-follower should aspire. For without it, we can't fulfill Christ's command to "love your enemies and pray for those who persecute you, so that you may be children of your Father in heaven" (Matt. 5:44–45).

Any relationship worth having is worth honoring. Our understanding of four Greek words for love helps us understand how to show honor in the various relationships throughout our lives. Therefore, love illuminates us to the role relationships fulfill in the life of a Christian.

The indigenous people of Northern America believed that culture was created through shared memory. In other words, the healthier your memories, the stronger your culture. Each relationship, whether it be a family, a circle of friends, a church, a job, or so on will have its distinctive elements. That is to say, through relating well, we build culture through the shared activities and moments that make up our memories. If memories are building blocks, then culture is itself the actual building. The greatest way to formulate healthy relationships is to know how to love well and always choose honor. Love and honor are the prisms by which we view the pursuit of healthy relationships. Therefore, in a relational sense, love and honor light the way for all the pragmatics of relationships. The truly virtuous person knows the value love and honor, and pursues this pathway toward the healthiest relationships possible. They realize the healthier one is relationally, the more human we become and the more we resemble and reflect our original design and purpose. In Christ, we can seek after our original purpose of relating well, for he enables us to be fully human in a world that seems to increasingly devalue human life.

6

Attitude

Step 6: Calibrate the Mentality of Your Heart

If anything, Nicholas Winton proves that ordinary people with extraordinary attitudes can change the brokenness of this world. Truth be known, the world wouldn't know his name were it not for a scrapbook created by a volunteer assistant all those years ago.

But I get ahead of myself.

The world was a powder keg in the mid-to-late-1930s, and Adolph Hitler's Third Reich seemed all too happy to provide both the powder and the match to light it. Rarely before has a word become so synonymous with evil as the term *Nazi*. Before his rise to power, few believed that Hitler was more than a ranting evil lunatic appealing to an uninformed, disgruntled, or sadistically misguided faction of the general population. After all, the Nazi party was young and had only formed from 1919 to 1922 following World War I. Their leading platform was driven by a type of nationalism that was extremely racist. Furthermore, they sought to eradicate communism and establish a system of national socialism. As insane as it may sound today, on January 30, 1933, Adolf Hitler was democratically elected chancellor of Germany through the nation's governmental structure. He burned, killed, outlawed, consolidated, and viciously bullied his way to a dictatorship from that point onward. The wave of the Third Reich was crashing against the shores of any German opponent as he positioned his new regime to fulfill his vision for the future. As Dietrich Bonhoeffer wrote, it was a "spectacle of a civilized society disintegrating into barbarianism."[1]

But this story isn't about Hitler. This is about Nicholas Winton.

In 1938, Nicholas Winton was a successful businessman working as a broker for the London Stock Exchange. He followed in his father's footsteps, who likewise had enjoyed a very successful career in banking. His family was of German-Jewish ancestry and had immigrated to England at the turn of the century. At age twenty-nine, he was single and excited about a two-week vacation during the Christmas holidays. He and a friend, Martin Blake, had planned to spend the time skiing in Switzerland.

Like so many others at that time, the two men watched as Germany became a society disintegrating into barbarianism. Martin had gone to Czechoslovakia and observed the mass amounts of displaced Jewish families due to that country's German occupation. He extended an invitation to his friend Winton to join him. This request and Winton's response would be the groundswell of what would come to be a worthy and world-changing cause.

In the refugee camps surrounding Prague, a significant problem emerged that galvanized a group of volunteers, that included Winton. It became their single focus in the months and days leading up to the beginning of World War II. While there were programs well underway to rescue Jewish children from Germany and Austria, there was no similar effort for Czechoslovakia's children. To this end, a small group of volunteers organized and strategized to create a way for Czech children who were Jewish to escape the Third Reich's evil wave that would soon come crashing down on that country.

There are times in history where the immediate needs cannot wait on governmental assistance or certain committees to take up a cause. Thus, before he was even granted permission, Winton established the Children's Section of the already-established British Committee for Refugees from Czechoslovakia. He even set up an office and began to meet with families eager to find a way to save their children from the impending doom they so feared. Thousands of families responded as applications were processed. Winton spent a month in Prague before returning to Britain to continue the work. Six weeks later, Germany occupied Czechoslovakia, and time was now a luxury Jewish families and children could no longer afford.

With the operation running at maximum capacity, Winton was doing everything he could to secure safe passage for as many children as possible. This included bribes when necessary in Prague to keep the authorities from asking too many questions about the thousands of families seeking help. Back in Britain, he took children's names to British authorities to ensure entry to the country. Furthermore, he secured foster homes for each child, organized and arranged trains, and raised the expenses to transport the children, and when there weren't enough funds, he paid from his personal account. On more than one occasion, documents were forged to transport children out of Prague and into Britain. Winton's daughter wrote concerning this aspect of her dad's personality: "Having quickly discovered how slowly bureaucratic committees can progress, he was determined that working outside them would facilitate his aims."[2]

The first transport was about twenty children and, by all indications, was the only time a plane was used to bring the children to Britain. From March to August, eight more transports, all by train, carried children away to safety. In August, three trains transported children, including one that brought 241, the largest number to date in the operation. A ninth transport was scheduled for September 1, 1939. The date came, and 250 children prepared to board. Sadly, this was also the day that Germany invaded Poland, and all borders were closed. Two days later, Britain declared war on Germany. The train was thus canceled. It is believed that nearly all the children scheduled to be on the ninth train died during the war, most of them in concentration camps.

All in all, Nicholas Winton saved 669 children from the Holocaust. Very few would ever see their parents again and were raised by their adopted families. After serving in the war, he continued to rebuild war-torn Europe through his banking profession. He fell in love with Grete Gjelstrup, a Danish woman who was an accountant while working in Paris. The two were married in October of 1948. Nicholas and Grete had three children and, by all accounts, deeply loved each other. Grete died on August 28, 1999 with two of her children holding her hands. Nicholas had gone home for the night to sleep. When he awoke, he was given the sad news that the fifty-three-year love affair had ended.

Remember the scrapbook?

When the war broke out, the operation to rescue children came to a close. Nine months of working at a fever pitch and to the point of exhaustion suddenly stopped. This was when a volunteer named Mr. W. M. Loewinsohn gathered all the data, including names, pictures, correspondence, and anything else relevant to their activities, and put them together in a scrapbook. The scrapbook was then presented to Nicholas Winton as a memento of all that they had accomplished together.

It was a beautiful gift, but one that would collect dust for nearly fifty years. It was eventually placed in the attic of the Wintons' home. Nicholas didn't speak of his efforts to rescue the children; thus, there were hundreds of children who had no idea who or how they had been rescued in those fateful months leading up to the war. One day Grete was up in the attic and came across the scrapbook. Taken aback by how well the efforts had been chronicled, she thought it might help those attempting to retrace the lives lost during World War II. She eventually connected with a Holocaust researcher who was married to a man involved in the media. The story found its way to a popular BBC television show where, in 1988, Nicholas Winton was invited to be part of a studio audience. He had no idea that night that the rest of the audience were part of the children, now in their fifties and sixties, whom he had rescued so many years earlier. The scrapbook was discussed by the host of the show *That's Life*, and then the emotional moment came when the audience was identified to Nicholas and Grete. It was the first time these children learned of the person who had saved their lives.

Nicholas Winton received worldwide recognition following the television show. He was given honors, a planet was named after him, the highest honor possible by the

Czechoslovakian government, and he was knighted by the Queen. But the limelight and attention was never something he sought out or, at times, enjoyed. He mostly spoke of the other volunteers who also worked so tirelessly to save the children. You see, it really was about the children. It was about tackling what seemed like an impossible task simply because it needed to be done. Because of the 669 documented children Nicholas Winton helped rescue, there are now more than 6,000 people alive today. Winton was known to his friends and family as "Nicky"; those he has rescued call themselves "Nicky's Children."

During the nine-month struggle to effect change and save the children, Nicky began to articulate what would become his life's mantra: "If something is not impossible, then there must be a way to do it." After observing so many children in harm's way and knowing that there was another environment where they could be safe, he meant that the seemingly impossible was actually possible. Just because the way is hidden doesn't mean it isn't there. Just because a madman has an army doesn't mean he can't be opposed. And just because no one else has figured out a way to save the Czech Jewish children living in refugee camps doesn't mean that a solution can't be found. And it didn't require a hero or heroine. The injustice simply needed someone with good character and the right attitude. An attitude that continually believed, "there must be a way." This is why Nicky would disagree with anyone who referred to him as great throughout the rest of his life. He lived to be 106 and died in 2015.[3]

Attitude: The Heart's Mentality

The world doesn't need more heroes or larger-than-life figures. It doesn't need more leaders who are so focused on personal branding that you couldn't find dirt underneath their fingernails with a microscope. It doesn't necessarily need another personality or social media sensation. Our world does need people who are more concerned with character than personality. Individuals with the right attitude, unphased by popularity and likability, who are deeply worried about the right intent overflowing to the right living. This is why the subject of attitude is so important. Attitude, when correctly understood, fundamentally impacts our relationships, decision-making, happiness at work or school, our trustworthiness, a commitment to excellence, and the list could go on and on. In short, our attitude will have an impact on the entirety of our lives. Oh, that we would have the attitude of Nicholas Winton, who believed *if something is not impossible, then there must be a way to do it.*

Okay, but first, what is "attitude"?

In short, our attitude is our inner disposition as displayed by the outer posture and position of our beings. It is the spirit, the persona of a person, produced from the correlation of the heart and mind. In an earlier chapter, we discussed this correlation. The heart and mind are, in one sense, inseparable. In other words, what I think about determines my feelings, and my feelings many times determine my actions. Likewise, my feelings may have a fundamental impact on what my mind focuses on, also determining my actions. It is best to think of the mind and heart by focusing on the conjunction "and." This little conjunction makes the attitude function healthy or unhealthy. The heart and mind work in tandem. What affects one impacts the other. Thus, *our attitudes can best be defined as the mentality of our hearts.*

Attitude is essential for virtuous living because it was a gift from God when we were made new creations in Christ. Paul speaks of this when he writes: "For God has not given us a *spirit* of fear, but one of power, love, and sound judgment" (2 Tim. 1:7, emphasis added). The word *spirit* is not the Holy Spirit, but rather the work of the Holy Spirit in our lives. Our spirit, or disposition, is comparable to the Greek word *charisma,* which means "a gift of grace."[4] Therefore, our attitude is a gift of grace given by the Holy Spirit, thus creating a spirit of power, love, and a sound mind.[5]

Now, let's be clear about something. Just because it is a gift doesn't mean we automatically have great attitudes. It is a gift that we must recognize and pursue every day! How sad is it to have been given so great a gift, only to let it lay dormant? A dormant gift of grace is an opportunity for the enemy and the old man (self) to determine one's attitude. But this gift, when utilized, holds the power for us to think and feel and thus act in a way that people "may see your good works and give glory to your Father in heaven" (Matt. 5:16).

Attitude: The Potential for Good or Bad

There is an ATTITUDE that PRECEDES every ACTION.

Think about that for a moment before reading any further. Behind every action is an attitude or the spirit of a person, which, as we have seen, is the mentality of one's heart.

Therefore, no action can be divorced from one's attitude. That makes my attitude a powerful force for good or bad in my life. If I have a bad attitude, then it casts a dark shadow across my heart and mind. But if I have a healthy attitude, the kind Paul describes as the gift of a spirit of love, power, and sound judgment . . . then it helps to focus my mind and affections on God and his purposes. It could be stated this way: *if the spirit of Christ dwells in you, then the spirit of Christ will shine through you.*

Now, let's be awkwardly honest about something here: this kind of attitude is countercultural. I mean, we don't post a picture or story hoping no one likes it. We want to accumulate hearts and thumbs up and expressive emojis; we want to have a following and, to many of us, brand matters deeply. Most people who are intentional with their lives aspire to be seen as a leader worth following, or at least a voice worth listening to. And these aren't necessarily bad things. But we have to continually check ourselves and ask: Is what's shining through the real you? And by the "real" you, I mean the you that was made new. Am I projecting based on a spirit of love, power, and sound judgment? You see, the most casual of actions—say a post with friends on a group date or a selfie before a big night out—can seem harmless enough. But even casual actions need to be motivated from the right attitude. Because if not, then we aren't rightly motivated and thus living by faith.

> All a person's ways seem right to him, but the
> Lord weighs motives. (Prov. 16:2)

> . . . everything that is not from faith is sin.
> (Rom. 14:23)

Jesus emphatically demonstrates how the attitude of the heart determines the actions of life in the beginning portions of the Sermon on the Mount. From Matthew 5:21–48, Jesus takes a countercultural approach to six specific subjects: murder and anger, immorality and lust, divorce, deceitful oaths, revenge and retaliation, and not hating your enemies. It was a countercultural approach because there was such emphasis among the Pharisees and other Jewish leaders on outward actions. The powerful were dictating the should-be-performance of the people, and something was missing.

Whenever we begin with performance, the original purpose gets lost. For so long, the crowds had heard an ever-growing list of what they should and should not do. Many probably even wondered if they were performing enough to be considered faithful. The Pharisees were a group or sect that had dedicated themselves to safeguarding, teaching, and observing the Mosaic laws. This sounds great at first glance, and many of them were undoubtedly simply striving for the pious life with good intentions. But the Pharisees had interpreted the law more important than the law itself. This means they viewed oral law with as much authority as the Mosaic laws. Oral law was "all the explanatory and supplementary material produced by, and contained within the oral tradition."[6] We begin to see the problem here: the Old Testament law never changes, but the oral law is continually evolving and growing. This leads to religion with basic laws and hundreds of others being added through interpretation and oral tradition over time. One can see how this can become maddening for the average Jew trying to live well and honor God with his or her life.

In the midst of this maddening approach to living . . . Jesus SIMPLIFIES everything!

And . . . Jesus still simplifies life for us today.

He addresses each of the six subjects with, "you have heard that it was said . . ." This is clearly a reference to the Pharisees' interpretation, or oral tradition, as it had exponentially grown through the years. Over and over again, Jesus demonstrates to his audience that life is not about adhering to lists. Coming through loud and clear to his listeners that day was a refreshing message they had never heard: *you don't have to perform to be accepted.*

Jesus isn't looking to make us behave a certain way. We are not puppets. Nor are we clones mindlessly following orders. We are thinking, feeling, infinitely valuable beings created in the very image of our Creator. But we are broken through and through. We aren't just damaged; we are dead from the inside out. This is why Jesus' message was so revolutionary. Life doesn't begin with performing, rather being transformed. And so time and time again, Jesus goes beyond the outer actions that we have heard so much about and deals with the source of our actions, the heart.

Jesus is demonstrating for a giant crowd that included those present that day and those of us who have joined in ever since: "Love, therefore, is the fulfillment of the law" (Rom. 13:10). As the lists of do's and don'ts continued to grow, Jesus taught that every part of a life worth living can be lived with a singular focus on love. Jesus is the love of God with skin on, who came to the earth to show us the way out of the sinful clutter of our own doing. His message, then and now, is to let the love of God in, and then the love of God will shine through your living.

Our heart's mentality, the spirit of our inner being, is a gift that includes a recipe of love, power, and sound judgment. Therefore, in so many ways, our attitude is the key to living this refreshing life with a sacredly simplistic focus. Virtuous living begins with a righteous being.

A Warning: Avoiding Cain's State of Mind

The first subject Jesus dealt with is actually the first crime committed in the Bible: murder. Quick Bible history lesson:

- Adam and Eve sin, thus destroying their relationship with God and getting kicked out of the garden of Eden.
- "The man was intimate with his wife Eve, and she conceived and gave birth to Cain" (Gen. 4:1).
- Soon Eve gave birth to her second son and named him Abel.
- Cain was an agriculturist and farmed the ground for fruits and vegetables, while Abel was a shepherd of flocks.
- "In the course of time Cain presented some of the land's produce as an offering to the LORD. And Abel also presented an offering—some of the firstborn of his flock and their fat portions. The LORD had regard for Abel and his offering, but he did not have regard for Cain and his offering. *Cain was furious, and he looked despondent*" (Gen. 4:3–5, emphasis added).
- Cain invites Abel to go with him out into the fields, where he then murdered him.

See what happened here? Cain was angry, furious in fact, and that impacted his outward appearance and eventually his actions. Violent hands begin with angry hearts. Cain's feelings became Cain's actions. The anger in his heart caused him to devalue the sanctity of human life and led him down a homicidal path.

This is why Jesus takes the commandment "Do not murder" and says, "But I tell you, everyone who is angry with his brother or sister will be subject to judgment" (Matt. 5:21–22). Jesus is taking a singular aim at the source of murder by focusing on any murderous or angry attitudes. Jesus knows that if the mentality of the heart is rightly focused, then, the murderous act never happens. We know that murder is a matter of the heart. If the mentality of the heart is anger, and that anger rages and burns like a fire, then it consumes life. In other words, if the heart's mentality is anger, then it has set itself on a path toward no regard for human life.

The flip side of the coin leads to a beautiful outcome: *if eternal life lives inside you, then human life is forever important to you.* Abel gave the best or "some of the firstborn of his flocks," while Cain gave an average gift or "some of the land's produce." Abel demonstrated gratitude that all good things come from God. Cain seemed to believe that everything he worked for was the result of his work ethic and ability. A blessing is never earned; it is undeserved . . . that's what makes it a blessing. Abel saw his flocks and knew God had blessed him; Cain looked at his work and might have thought he was the blessing to God. In any case, the mentality of his heart was flawed and, thus, it had a devastating impact.

We are all just one thought away from a Cain state of mind. This is a challenge for so many, particularly those who live in the United States. There is an individualistic-ness woven into our historical and cultural DNA. We are proud of what we can accomplish. We look at our country and think God blessed us because we worked so hard and were founded on Judeo-Christian values. There is some truth to this. But our history is littered with injustices that would seemingly disqualify us from any blessing from God. From slavery to Jim Crow laws to civil rights . . . from women getting the right to vote just in the last hundred years to *Roe v. Wade* and millions of lives being killed in the womb . . . from drug addiction and the opioid crisis to a social media age that finds us addicted to everything from fake news to semipornographic reels. If anything, our history is a mixed bag, and we are a shining example of God blessing and undeserving people.

Don't get me wrong. I love my country and am a proud patriot of it. I believe the citizens of our country are capable of being the bravest, smartest, most compassionate people on the planet. But the Cain state of mind lurks around every corner. We can never take credit for last year's harvest when it was God who brought the rains. We can never fall prey to, "Look what we did! Of course, we deserve to be blessed!" The mentality of our hearts should be, "Look how God has blessed. I am going to love well today so that others may be blessed."

In the end, regretful actions happen when we fail to pursue righteousness inwardly. And yet, God has granted us everything necessary through the person and work of Jesus Christ and the Holy Spirit in our lives to adjust the mentality of our hearts daily. The entirety of one's being marinates in the spirit of that person. The attitude given to people who follow Jesus is like a light illuminating a dark room, every corner, every crevice, every part. Thus, if one has a positive spirit, a

Jesus-honoring tone to their existence, every other virtue discussed in this book becomes more doable. We must only look to Jesus daily. As the English poet Frederick Langbridge wrote:

> Two men look out through the same bars;
> One sees the mud and the other the stars.

God has given us Jesus, but he will not force us to look upon him. Our heart's mentality can never be properly calibrated unless our gaze is fixed upon the one who changes us from the inside out.

Thousands of people today believe they are part of Sir Nicholas Winton's family. Some view themselves as grandchildren or great-grandchildren. Some still simply go by the affectionate phrase, "Nicky's Children." His name has become their name, and the lives he rescued are filled with gratitude. We also are part of a big family where the table of grace is growing by the day. The name of Jesus has become our name in that we are called sons and daughters of God. We are God's children, and we are grateful.

7

Worthiness

Step 7: Construct a Moral Vision for Your Future

Worth

There is a truth that often gets twisted. Some are too careful not to say it in a way that seemingly detracts from God's glory. Others overemphasize it, negating God's glory and thus elevating humanity too much. In either case, here it is:

> You are forever important to God; *you* are infinitely valuable.

Think about it this way. People are the only thing God created that will last forever. And since the story of Adam and Eve is really the story of us, we should take great comfort that humans are the pinnacle of God's creation.

I was recently sitting at a conference that I helped lead, which took place in London, England. The night's distinguished guest was Dr. John Lennox. The audience consisted of several hundred students from all over the United States going through our Student Leadership University journey. Dr. Lennox is a mathematician, philosopher, and one of the leading Christian apologists in the world. He teaches at one of the colleges for Oxford University, and, fun fact, his time there overlapped by a few years with C. S. Lewis.

Nevertheless, having our students sit under his tutelage one evening was a rare treasure that no one took lightly. I remember that night clearly; he was sharing his research on the ethics of AI (Artificial Intelligence) and how the domination of technology is changing who we are. At one point, he explained how all of creation shows God's glory, but it isn't made in his image. He then casually shared how he liked to go out in his garden and look through his telescope at the stars and galaxies. Dr. Lennox then named one that was his favorite galaxy to observe. He quit speaking for a few seconds, which felt like minutes, and then stated in a thick Irish accent: "You know you are more valuable to God than a galaxy."

As you can imagine, there was a long, reflective pause following the statement. I have pondered that statement so many times since. God created us to have worth that exceeds entire galaxies. Our worth to God cannot be measured against anything temporal that wasn't created in his image.

Yet, even when we rebelled and treated God as worthless . . . he still saw worth in us. Broken, but still just as valuable. Our worth had not diminished, but our ability to approach God was destroyed. Nothing that God created was valuable enough or worthy enough to heal this brokenness. So God sent his Son Jesus, who has existed from eternity past, to redeem us and transform us from worth to worthy of a relationship with God again. We are infinitely valuable to God, and it took God's infinite love for us to have a way back to him. It looks something like this:

- We were created with infinite worth.
- We severed our relationship with God but never lost our value to him.
- Jesus is the only worthy sacrifice for the sins of mankind.
- Jesus transforms us from having worth to being worthy of a relationship with God again.
- Therefore, we live worthy because we have been made worthy.

"The Times They Are a-Changin'": The Need for a Moral Vision

There are many aspects of our lives in which we must seek to be worthy, in which we must live up to the worthiness we have in Jesus. But for the purposes of Step 7 we are focusing on worthiness as it pertains to sexual morality. A dictionary definition of *worthiness* is "the quality of being good enough; suitability." In our case, worthiness is a description of the moral courage necessary to pursue the type of decency that glorifies Christ. It is recognizing that, though I am infinitely valuable in my worth to God, my sin meant I was never good enough to get back into a relationship with God. And then Jesus changed all that.

Because Jesus is enough = I am now enough
(i.e., worthiness)

A moral vision creates within us a daily realization that we are going to live worthy of Jesus concerning anything that relates to our sexuality. Or as Paul taught Titus: "instructing us to deny godlessness and worldly lusts and to live in a sensible, righteous, and godly way in the present age" (Titus 2:12). Bob Dylan famously once wrote "The Times They Are a-Changin'" as the title track to his third studio album. Truer words have never been used to describe the evolution or de-evolution of sexuality in the digital era in which we now live. Therefore, a clear moral vision has never been more critical.

To begin with, we must dispel the myth that we are on a journey of self-discovery. And that, at some point in the future, a full picture will be unearthed, leaving us standing proud and saying, "HERE I AM . . . I HAVE DISCOVERED MYSELF AND THIS IS ME!" I hear parents all the time say, "He or she is just trying to find themselves." I often listen to individuals describe their own lives in terms of the journey toward self. But the greatest discovery that can be made is that we are not created to discover ourselves; God created us to discover him, and to know and enjoy him.

Yes, we journey, but not to discover ourselves. We journey because we are going home to the heaven country. Self-discovery is simply something that happens along the way. And even before we arrive in heaven, we must "walk worthy of God, who calls you into his own kingdom and glory" (1 Thess. 2:12). The point is to discover how I can do everything within my ability to live worthy of God. Along the way, we need to find our talents and gifts, our personalities and preferences. But finding self is never the endgame. Any discovery about self is only a tool of living worthy. In reality, the greatest discovery about self will not happen until we reach heaven, and God has made all things forever new.

The question then becomes how my worthiness can determine my view and conduct in regard to my sexuality. *Sexuality* is a very broad term that can refer to anything from sexual feelings to orientation to activity. Our sexuality can be understood to have three dimensions: our hearts and minds (*what we think about, the images that catch and consume our mind's eye*); our hands and actions (*the expression of our sexuality*); and our relationships (*how our sexuality contributes to relationships*). Our goal now is not to address every issue regarding sexuality at the crossroads of faith and culture. But we will focus on God's ideal for our lives and the tools necessary to live with a single-mindedness toward the best version of our sexuality.

A moral vision begins with a deeply held belief in the gospel. Jesus transformed us and, in so doing, granted us worthiness by which to live. If I am enough in Jesus, then moral courage should characterize my approach to sexuality. Sexual morality will require courage, grit, and determination to never give up or give in—a refusal to compromise our moral integrity. When Jesus uttered one word on the cross, which translates into three English words, "It is finished," he meant that the sin debt of all mankind had been paid in full. Therefore, our virtue isn't for sale to any ungodly circumstance or temptation that may arise because our debt has been paid.

Let's then ask ourselves: What is the moral vision for my life? Future casting the type of person you wish to be based on your worthiness in Jesus is necessary. For if a moral vision is not firmly established and pursued, then the darker angels of our old self will seek to determine our identity.

"This Is the Way": The Components of a Moral Vision

I'm a Star Wars nerd and I don't even try to hide it. As I write these very words, a Chewbacca stuffed animal that makes his distinct sound when squeezed is sitting on the corner of my desk watching this manuscript unfold. I also think the new Star Wars series *The Mandalorian* is spectacular. I mean, how can you go wrong when Jon Favreau is in charge of a project? In a galaxy with an eclectic assortment of alien races and planets, *The Mandalorian* takes place several years after the fall of the empire in *Return of the Jedi*. At this point in galactic history, Mandalorians were fierce and feared warriors. As one of the series characters described them, "Mandalorian isn't a race. It's a Creed." They were known for following a strict code often invoked by their mantra, "This is the way." The way is simply the code by which they lived, including never removing your helmet in front of anyone.

As we outline a moral vision for our future, we are stating clearly, "This is who I am going to be . . . this is the way." As followers of Jesus, we adhere to a code that has always been a sexual counterculture. Dating back to the earliest chapters of church history and the days of the Roman Empire, sex was viewed very differently. Pastor and author Tim Keller explains:

> Roman culture insisted that married women of social status abstain from sex outside of marriage, but it was expected that men (even married men) would have sex with people lower on the status ladder—slaves, prostitutes, and children. This wasn't only allowed; it was regarded as unavoidable. This was in part

because sex in that culture was always considered an expression of one's social status. Sex
was mainly seen as a mere physical appetite
that was irresistible. . . .[1]

On the other hand:

Christians' sexual norms were different, of
course. The church forbade any sex outside of
heterosexual marriage. . . . It saw sex not just
as an appetite but as a way of giving oneself
wholly to another and, in so doing, imitate
and connect to the God who gave himself in
Christ. It also was more egalitarian, treating
all people as equal and rejecting the double
standards of gender and social status. Finally,
Christianity saw sexual self-control as an exercise of human freedom, a testimony that we
aren't mere pawns of our desires or fate.[2]

The times have changed, and the challenges regarding
sexuality have grown more and more complicated. The lines
that clearly shouldn't be crossed in one chapter of history seem
erased at other times. Sin confuses everything. And yet, just
when things couldn't get more complicated and confusing,
God in his goodness is saying, "This is the way."

A moral vision for the future begins with the understanding that God created us as sexual beings and, therefore, sex
was his idea. If God created it, then it was good and fulfilled
a good purpose, which brings us to the other components of
a moral vision. The creation narrative, along with other places
in Scripture, teaches us that the gift of sex is to be enjoyed

between a man and a woman within the holy relationship called marriage. Sex between a married couple furthers several main purposes.

A beautiful and God-honoring event happens when a married couple "become one flesh" (Gen. 2:24) through sexual union. The two that become one demonstrates for us, as Keller pointed out, a countercultural approach to sexuality. First, "both people, while remaining *two* as creatures of God, become *one* body, that is, belong to one another in love."[3] That man and woman would leave their parents and bond with one another, communicates complete oneness and faithfulness to the other. They are man and woman, two individuals joined together in love, and they are meant to stay unwaveringly faithful to the highest possible degree of their belonging to each other.[4] In addition to the purity and beauty of intimate oneness, sex was also given to us for the purposes of building families, pleasure, and guarding ourselves against sexual sin.

The intimacy shared between husband and wife is a spiritual unity: "Therefore, what God has joined together, let no one separate" (Matt. 19:6). And it is also a powerful analogy of the love and faithfulness that exists between God and his people. Scripture refers to the people of God, the church, as the bride, and Jesus as the bridegroom. Marriage should be a small preview of coming attractions pointing to the one-day union of God and his people in heaven. In that sense, the church should seek to remain pure and holy. In other words, there will be a day when we will hear these words: "Let us be glad, rejoice, and give him glory, because the marriage of the Lamb has come, and his bride has prepared herself" (Rev. 19:7).

There is no greater motivation for crafting a moral vision for our future than realizing *when two become one, their love echoes the beauty of God's future heavenly handiwork.* Our love here and now can point to a day when God will restore and make all things new again. Our moral vision can be inspired by and evidence of God's ultimate vision for his people he redeems and will one day restore.

The Romans were undoubtedly spot-on in their assessment that a sexual appetite was a strong passion. But they were wrong to believe that sexual appetites can be satisfied in a myriad of ways. Let's think about it this way. If I let my kids eat junk food and fast food for every meal, their unhealthy appetite grows. They want more combinations of flavors in their chips, more greasy French fries, and more candy. After all, sugar is very addictive and, when overconsumed, can cause addicts to look for their next sugar-high or dopamine release. On the other hand, if my children eat healthy foods involving fruits and vegetables, they train their palate to want healthy meals. When it came to their sexuality, the Romans were like kids on a steady diet of junk food. This led to more depraved flavors of how they satisfied their sexual appetites. No one would argue that the world has grown more complicated since the time of the Romans.

What is so freeing is that in the midst of an over-sexualized culture . . .

- a culture that sexualizes children and seemingly everything else
- a society that equates sexual inclination with identity
- a social media era that ensures sexual images will ensnare the wandering eye

- a world with a new worldly appetite appearing on the horizon daily

There is a sacredly simple idea, a moral vision, through which we can filter all our passions, desires, questions, and inclinations. In a complicated world, God gives us clarity. In confusing times, God invites us to take refuge and comfort in his purposes.

Realize this isn't confining; rather, it is liberating. If the garden of Eden taught us anything, it's that *more experience doesn't give me a better experience*. God didn't want them to eat of the tree in the middle of the garden. In consuming the fruit, their sin ruined life as they knew it. Once they ate the forbidden fruit, they became slaves to sin, as did we all. God gave us freedom, and we chose what was forbidden. God's vision for our sexuality is freedom to love and be loved as he intended. Sure, there is so much outside of that vision that is forbidden. Rebellious people will always find numerous ways to invent more junk food to eat. And all along, God is whispering through the endless image-fueled algorithms and messages reinforcing a different version of sexuality: *come and be redeemed; come and be free.*

With that in mind, here are four questions to ask as we seek to live our worthiness in a world of misguided perceptions:

1. Am I stewarding my sexuality to demonstrate my worthiness? Am I entertaining sexual feelings and/or sexual actions inconsistent with the Scriptures' moral vision for sexuality?
2. If single, am I preparing myself to become one flesh with my future spouse?

3. If unmarried, am I remaining pure, realizing that my purity reflects the manner in which God wants to present his people (the bride) to Jesus (the bridegroom)?
4. If married, am I demonstrating worthiness in my thoughts, feelings, and activities? Am I pursuing my spouse selflessly, frequently, and satisfactorily?

RUN and Don't Apologize or Compromise: Guarding the Moral Vision

Moral excellence necessitates a steadfast and fervent commitment to God's vision for sexuality. This is why Jesus used such strong language in his Sermon on the Mount when he preached:

> ". . . everyone who looks at a woman lustfully has already committed adultery with her in his heart. If your right eye causes you to sin, gouge it out and throw it away. For it is better that you lose one of the parts of your body than for your whole body to be thrown into hell. And if your right hand causes you to sin, cut it off and throw it away. For it is better that you lose one of the parts of your body than for your whole body to go into hell." (Matt. 5:28–30)

Jesus isn't subtle regarding moral integrity. First, Jesus is not saying that self-mutilation is a reasonable strategy for living your worthiness. This is an obvious case of hyperbole. If sexual immorality begins in the mind and heart, then amputation isn't the answer.

What Jesus is teaching us is that any and all sexual immorality is outside of the moral vision he wants for our lives. The individual seeking to live his or her worthiness aims only at the highest ideals for life. This means that compromise isn't an option. It is hard to compromise once, somewhat difficult the second time, and easier the third. One way of thinking about it is that the Christian is an idealist in every sense. Another way of saying it is that compromising our moral integrity in any way can destroy us. When we compromise, we are dancing with the devil to a slow song, and when the music stops . . . we are in hell on the earth.

Paul warned the Corinthian church:

> Flee sexual immorality! Every other sin a person commits is outside the body, but the person who is sexually immoral sins against his own body. Don't you know that your body is a temple of the Holy Spirit who is in you, whom you have from God? You are not your own, for you were bought at a price. So glorify God with your body. (1 Cor. 6:18–20)

It is clear that we fight through or flee from anything inconsistent with worthiness. And in fleeing, we are not retreating. Instead, we are simply moving forward, running toward a better vision. You see, the moral courage it takes to run away from immorality means we have to play offense and defense simultaneously. And in so doing, every breath declares the belief that we are enough in Jesus.

Many of us are reading these words with a less than worthy past. Many of us have emotional scars from past regrets. And some of us feel like our pasts are so littered with mistakes that they have come to define us. Indeed, sexual sin often carries lasting consequences. Likewise, the shame and guilt of yesterday frequently become the invisible prison of today and tomorrow. One of the enemy's greatest strategies is to keep us focused on our imperfect past. You see, when we focus on our past mistakes, we judge ourselves on our failures. But a moral vision is about our worthiness in the present and all future moments because of Christ's sufficiency. Knowing and believing this transforms our perspective. We understand that God doesn't judge us by past mistakes, but according to the redemptive work of Jesus. The best moment in anyone's life is when the great miracle of salvation happens. What a liberating idea, then, that because of Jesus, we are not judged by our worst moments . . . but by the single greatest moment in our lives.

The Rose That No One Wanted

*There was once a rose that grew in the shade of
an oak*

*It would soak the right amount of sun, then rest
in the shade of a caring cloak*

*One day the rose was picked, earlier than it
was ever meant to be caught*

*Taken from the towering oak, prematurely
before the time it ought*

*Petals partially showing . . . color a glimpse of
glowing*

*Its beholder inextricably drawn to the beauty of
the thing*

*Not fully understanding the consequence in the
moment*

*The fate of the rose's glory now hostage to time
already spent*

*At first the rose was flattered, certainly there
was splendor to behold*

*Too much splendor . . . for the rose went from
something beholden to constantly being held*

*For a time the petals blossomed with vibrant
color*

*But the seemingly endless bliss soon took a
detour*

*The rose soon found that with each touch,
petals blackened and decayed*

*Soon it was discovered that majesty had passed,
leaving it dismayed*

*Deteriorated and exposed, the rose had no hope
for tomorrow*

*After all, how can one have hope when all that
exists is sorrow?*

*It would appear the story of the rose was over
before it began*

*Before long the rose would be discarded, as it is
with all things no one wants*

*Beauty robbed and deprived by those who look
and took without asking, the rose was cursed*

*In a bout of ostensible irony, the beholder one
night discarded the rose*

*There, the rose assumed, the end would come
like a dark poetic pose*

*Then . . . through the darkness . . . through the
pain . . . through the tears someone spoke*

*What the rose had mistaken as darkness was
actually the shadow of the oak*

*"Dear rose you have returned, you are now
home, but you are moving a little slow."*

*"Oh, oak of my youth, I haven't returned, I
have been tossed out to where the lost things go."*

*"Hmmm, interesting, share with me where you
have wandered."*

"I thought I had been chosen, but it turns out I was simply shared until no longer wanted."

"Hmmm, curious, so is this the end of the beautiful rose that grew in my shade?"

"This is undoubtedly the end, there is no one left who wants me . . . including myself!"

"Hmmm, fascinating, but my dear rose, the day is not gone.

For you see in the shadow of grace is where the lost things get found

Covered in the glory of my shade you are beautiful

Wrapped in my presence you are not a neighbor, you are family

Protected in my strength, you were not 'tossed out,' but returned, redeemed, and restored."

And with that, the rose breathed for the first time . . . and knew she was home.[5]

We are all the rose that was discarded. We all live in the shadow of God's grace . . . for that is where the lost things get found.

Living and Loving in an LGBTQIA+ World

With a clear moral vision that is sacredly simple in mind, we are then positioned to live and love in the beauty of God's desired will. This doesn't discount that some of us have very real feelings regarding our sexuality that are in contradiction to Scripture. The evolving abbreviation for those identifying with other versions of sexuality is L (lesbian) G (gay) B (bisexual) T (transgender) Q (queer or questioning) I (intersex) A (asexual). While not every abbreviation is found in the Bible, two prominent examples from the ancient world are: gay and lesbian.

The world we live in affords and celebrates the ability to "self-identify" based on one's proclivities and inclinations. But are feelings regarding sexuality a choice? For much of my life, I never questioned why someone would engage in, say, homosexual activity. The extent of my argument was that the Bible condemns those actions, and the person chooses to be the way he or she is. But what if attraction to people of the same sex can't be helped? What if that attraction is there without one's choosing or desiring it to be there? What if someone feels like a girl on the inside but has all the boy parts on the outside? What if someone is attracted to both sexes? I ask these questions because of my own inclination to be very heavy-handed in truth but not grace.

Since we have already seen God's desires for our sexuality, let's look at "gay" or "queer" as an example of how to think about all the abbreviations. While the Bible doesn't specifically mention intersex or transgender or asexual, our path is still illuminated on how to think about all the ways people self-identify through the example of "homosexuality." There are six references to homosexuality in the Bible, and in each reference, an action or desire of the mind (lust) or action of the hands (sexual activity) is addressed. In other words, *the Bible does not condemn homosexual inclination or attraction per se; the Scriptures do, however clearly condemn homosexual activity and lust.* That doesn't mean that all sexual orientations have the same moral equivalence. It simply points out that, since we are inclined to all kinds of sin, those inclinations don't necessarily determine identity.

Sexual orientation or inclination *does not determine* a person's identity.

Andrew Sullivan, a prominent thought leader on gay rights, defines the term to mean "someone who is constitutively, emotionally and sexually, attracted to the same sex."[6] William Lane Craig, a respected and accomplished Christian apologist, shares a similar definition when he writes, "being a homosexual is a state or an orientation; a person who has a homosexual orientation might not ever express that orientation in actions."[7] Others would take a different approach, looking to ongoing sexual activity as the defining characteristic of what it means to be gay.[8] Notice that the first two definitions focused on attraction and inclination while the third focused on activity. This then raises the question: Is homosexuality being or doing?

The gospel of grace means that when we make a declaration to follow Christ, our identity is transformed on all levels and we are saved to good works. As followers of Jesus, we don't find our identity in sexual orientation, but rather in Christ. Our identity begins with *being* made new in Christ and is evidenced in our *doing* the good works that God prepared for us ahead of time. To put it more bluntly: God won't judge you based on who you are or are not attracted to . . . but consequences are attached to how we respond to such attraction. Inclination and orientation do not determine who we become. And that is because of who I am in Jesus, and the expression of that new-creation identity, cannot be separated.

It may do us well to remember that some of our brothers and sisters are not sexually sinning, but rather suffering in their struggle with sexuality. Let's be honest: we all struggle with some aspect of our sexuality. The Greek word *porneia* is a broad term including all sexual immorality. This was a word that the apostle Paul used to describe the sexual immorality in the church at Corinth. All human beings who follow Jesus, with rare exceptions, will face temptations to compromise on the moral vision that we have adopted. The struggle is real for everyone; some struggles just run deeper because the cultural norm has equated sexuality with identity. Nevertheless, the person who looks at pornography in the dark corners of his or her life is just as guilty as the transgendered person expressing gender different from the one they were born with. And since the struggle is real for all, here are a few ways we can love one another well.

Understand Our Role to Be Abraham, Not God

There is a familiar event in Genesis 19 of God destroying the two cities on the plain of Jordan named Sodom and Gomorrah. These cities were famous for their sexual immorality and wickedness, with the Bible emphasizing homosexual promiscuity. It is clear that the cities' sin was immense and extremely serious. The city's men groped, molested, and sexually abused practically everything that moved or dared to enter the city. The city had already collapsed on itself because of its immorality. And once Lot and his family left, these two cities were death traps for any traveler. Nevertheless, God was slow to wrath and patient with Abraham who said, "Will you really sweep away the righteous with the wicked? What if there are fifty righteous people in the city? Will you really sweep it away . . ." God replied, "I will spare the whole place for their sake" (Gen. 18:23–24, 26). In this moment, Abraham realized he might have overshot his number and began to plea: Will you destroy it if there are forty-five righteous people? Forty? Thirty? Twenty? Ten? Each time Abraham appealed to God, the response was the same. Eventually, God did destroy the cities.

Usually, we have one of two responses to God destroying Sodom and Gomorrah. The first is confusion and a bit of disbelief. We think: *Really, how could God do such a thing?* Honestly, this was similar to Abraham's first reaction. But remember, God sees all things. He knows how the story of history's future will unfold, and "we know that all things work together for the good of those who love God, who are called according to his purpose" (Rom. 8:28). God has a story he is telling that ultimately desires for as many as possible to be redeemed. I hold on to these truths in the midst of confusion.

The second response is: *Well, they got what they deserved.* It is true that the sin of Sodom and Gomorrah sought to drown out any good in this world. It is also true that these cities had devalued life to something that was meant to satisfy a momentary sexual impulse. But it is wrong to think that the weight of such sins is heavier than others on the shoulders of Jesus as he hung, bled, and died on a cross suspended between heaven and earth.

This brings us to the proper response: to identify our role in this historic event. It should be obvious, the two main characters in the conversation were God and Abraham. Our role is to live and love well and plead for those who are so lost that they can't see the light. Our role is to be Abraham and trust God to, well, be the authority on all things. If, by some chance, we have assumed the wrong role, then let's stop trying to wear the God-hat. It doesn't fit our human heads anyway. Instead, let's start serving and preserving. Being Abraham might not always yield the results you want, but it is a hat that certainly fits.

Communicate the Truth about Sin as If It Pains Us

As we've already admitted, the biblical truth about sexuality can be a tough pill to swallow, especially for those in the midst of the struggle. That is why we must communicate the truth about sexuality outside of God's moral vision with care and compassion. In fact, we should only discuss the truth about such sinful ways when our hearts first break for sinners. Remember, sin fractures every human soul. We do not discuss such things with a badge of heterosexual honor. After all, we're not given a right standing before God because we are heterosexual versus any of the LGBTQIA+ abbreviations. You don't go to heaven because you fall in love with someone of the opposite sex. All that will matter when stepping into eternity is Jesus. In the meantime, another's pain should be met with patience. Compassion is not a compromise. So, we do not pridefully herald struggles with sexuality. Rather, we hurt with those who struggle and walk alongside them, showing hope for a better day.

Avoid Bumper Sticker and 280-Character Theology

Have you ever heard someone deliver an entire argument against LGBTQIA+ using only bumper sticker phrases such as "God didn't create Adam and Steve. He created Adam and Eve!"? This is why social media doesn't provide the best platform for such discussions. Social media doesn't offer us the proximity needed to encompass both truth and grace. It can be helpful in so many ways, but we must use it wisely. Back to our bumper sticker theology example: What's incorrect about the statement and approach is twofold.

First, the argument is incomplete—and this is where cute-sounding slogans posted on social media fail repeatedly. Like an air gun, they make a lot of noise, but there are no bullets, so they're ineffective in ever hitting the bull's-eye. To offer a complete biblical argument is to present a comprehensive moral vision that includes both truth and grace. It's important to remember that an incomplete argument or position is more likely to represent Satan; we only need to remember the fall of man to find evidence of this.

Second, the bumper-sticker argument is incorrect because it doesn't seem to represent the attitude of Christ. In my experience, the person who doesn't represent a Christlike attitude toward LGBTQIA+ is usually someone who will either laugh at an inappropriate joke or make jokes themselves regarding sexuality. However, depravity and unrighteousness are never laughing matters; in fact, they represent a sin for which many Christians need to repent.

As followers of Jesus, we are surrounded by people with many different orientations and inclinations. Our attitude could, in fact, determine the amount of influence we're able to have in this life and the one to come.

Love the Sinner, and Let's Hate Our Own Sin

All my life I've heard the statement: "Love the sinner and hate the sin." Some years ago, a pastor friend of mine started a Bible study in an art district. He did this because many young adults from his church lived in the area, making the Bible study within walking distance. The gatherings were very casual and involved some teaching, discussion, and a meal. It was a place for real and raw thoughts and feelings to be shared. All along, my friend carefully reinforced a moral vision that leads to freedom concerning our sexuality. He never went out of his way to do this, but when the subject came up, he didn't run from it.

At one point, a couple hundred people were attending the Bible study. Honestly, facilitating a meal for that many people was the most challenging part. Friendships were formed, community cultivated, and a culture solidified. One of the benefits of a culture built on the love of Jesus is that honest conversations can take place. After several months, there were quite a few people attending who were identified as LGBTQIA+. At this point, you might be wondering, *How did anyone know they were associated with the LGBT community?* Remember, when you genuinely love, you have real conversations about life.

Then one evening, sharing a meal around a table, my friend asked a question to a woman who regularly brought her girlfriend to the Bible study.

He said, "Would you mind if I asked a question just out of curiosity?"

She replied, "Sure!"

"Well, we get together once a week and study the Bible, and the other week someone asked a question about sexuality and marriage."

"Oh, I remember," she said, laughing a bit and glancing at her girlfriend.

"So my question is: Why didn't that scare you away? You didn't get mad; you didn't rant on social media about the church or Christianity. You showed up the next week to help set up chairs."

"You are asking me why I attend every week when a part of my life contradicts some of what you are saying?"

"I guess so," my friend said reluctantly.

"Honestly, it is pretty simple. When I was a kid, I went to church. As an adult, there is a part of me that misses it but doesn't feel comfortable walking into most churches."

"That makes sense," my friend replied.

"A coworker invited me to this gathering. At first, I was nervous. When I was a kid, the pastor used to say all the time, 'God loves the sinner but hates the sin!' So I guess that I had that voice bouncing around in my brain when I first attended. But soon after that, I realized something: these people seem to love the sinner and hate their sin."

She then looked very seriously at my pastoral friend and said, "And when I hear you teach, it seems that you truly love us and that God is still working on some of the broken pieces in your life."

Trying to hold back tears, my friend simply said, "Thank you," and then talked about something else.

When love is at the center of your motivation and life, then there is nothing to fear. Having a moral vision for your life gives you the freedom to live and love as Jesus would. And by loving well, we demonstrate God's kindness, which can lead to real and lasting change in someone's life! Love all the sinners—love them the way that Jesus would—and hate your sin, if you are going to hate anything.

We have worth, Jesus is worthy, and we have been given worthiness because we are redeemed. Every day God sings a sweet and clear song of his mercies over the entirety of his creation. Even in a mystifying world that seems to be consumed with sexuality confusing the narrative of identity—even still, the melody and lyrics of his goodness burst forth like the light of the day. It seems that a fog that can blur our worldview settles on the morning in an effort to fight the light and drown out God's song. But his song gives us a vision through it. While it's not always easy, this vision has a sacred clarity because of our worthiness. It requires us to be a people that muster up the moral courage to be . . . well . . . *moral*, to live our worth and "be content with the approval of Christ rather than with the false opinion of our flesh."[9] So live your worth. After all, you are more valuable to God than a galaxy.

8

Respect

Step 8: Build a Reputation of Honor

As we continue to seek after a less-cluttered life that is clean with a sacred simplicity, there must be a holy consistency across the entirety of our lives. As Oswald Chambers once wrote: "We are only what we are in the dark . . ."[1]

I have heard some attempt to teach that we must seek to be consistent with our public and private lives, our church and not-at-church selves, our school or work identities versus the one at home. This is rubbish of the highest degree. Your best life is not one where your character has a multiple personality disorder. The exhaustion so many of us suffer from is the result of trying too hard to be someone we were never intended to be. We are not actors on a stage. There is no stage. There are no lights. There is no audience. We are simply telling a story with our lives that has the Redeemer as the heroic character and redemption as the central theme.

If you have decided to leave behind the oft-familiar chaos and dysfunction mentioned above, you seek to walk down a road less traveled, one with sacred purpose. A reputation will then emerge that is as beautiful as the sunset over a snow-capped mountain and as refreshing as a spring breeze in a field of flowers. It will be a reputation known for building up in a world of tearing down, and seeking the good over the bad . . . a reputation of honor.

Think about it this way for a moment: Wouldn't it be nice *not* to feel the need to catch up on all the latest gossip headlines? Or scroll through social media, feeling inadequate? Or be concerned about what others think about that super-cool gray minivan you drive? Wouldn't it be nice *not* to feel like you're drowning in others' opinions or, rather, what is so many times our perception of others' opinions? Or struggle with all the parts of your life's puzzle not measuring up to a vision adopted based on culture? What if we could kick all that to the curb and live differently?

There is a remedy.

This approach to life that we are painting step after step is transforming. And one of the things it transforms is our perspective.

When we live seeking to respect through showing honor, there are no margins left for a cancerous attraction to the chaos that formerly consumed us.

Respect: "A Fellow of Good Respect . . . with a Smatch of Honor in It"

I've always been a fan of Shakespeare, though I readily admit that I couldn't understand his writings without the help of supplemental guides. Maybe what I like is the artful manner in which he crafts a story line more than his writing style.

Seriously, the guy wrote thirty-seven plays in twenty-three years, and that doesn't even include his collaborations with other artists. One of my favorites is *Julius Caesar*. Despite the play's title, the character of Brutus could be considered the main character. The entire play is tense from beginning to end. The story is set in Rome in 44 BC and revolves around Brutus joining a group of conspirators who want to assassinate Caesar, so he doesn't become a dictator. The aftermath following Caesar's death is as dramatic as the murder itself. It doesn't end well as the story line descends to civil war, suicides, defeats, and victories.

During the civil war, Brutus suffers defeat. Brutus then asks a loyal soldier named Strato to hold his sword to run himself through and commit suicide. In some of his final words, Brutus pays tribute to Strato before he takes his life: "Thou art a fellow of a good respect; Thy life hath had some smatch of honor in it." Though it seems cruel and unethical in our day, it was considered loving and honorable at certain points in history for leaders who had been defeated or captured to commit suicide. It was still considered a noble death if they could die with their own sword. Many times the leaders from the opposing army would allow this noble death to occur after capture. Other times, wartime leaders would commit suicide out of a sense of shame and failure. If they were created to lead an army to victory, and that army lost, then their lives had no value . . . or so goes the logic.

In any case, Strato was respectful and honorable, even to the end of Brutus' life. SparkNotes translates those final words this way: "You're a man with a good reputation. Your life has had honor in it. Then, hold my sword and turn your face away while I run on it. Will you, Strato?"[2] There is an enduring truth here that helps us further simplify our lives: *A life that is lived showing respect, in turn, creates a reputation for honoring other lives.*

Respect is a conscious decision to honor. A simple dictionary definition of respect is "an act of giving particular attention or consideration; high or special regard or the quality or state of being esteemed."[3] To respect someone is to show edifying attention to them by regarding that person as someone to be esteemed. As the great reformer John Calvin defined it, honor is "reverence shown with heart, mouth, and hand—in thought, word, and deed."[4]

Now, I know some of you might be thinking, *Respect and honor sound a lot like the same thing.* And while there is much overlap in the meaning of these two terms, I would like to point out why we are making a distinction with this step toward our best lives. Respect is something that can, possibly, be demonstrated outwardly, while not inwardly. But Calvin's definition of honor shows continuity between outward action and inward thoughts and feelings. And this is why we choose to use both words.

Think about it this way: respect is the what; honor is the how. By choosing our best life, we are deciding to respect all persons in our lives. We accomplish this decision to respect by honoring that person. The result is simply that over time we become the types of persons who have a good and godly reputation. It's a liberating thing to live without having to decide if we will or will not respect and, thus, honor someone. Because we are following Jesus and walking in the shadow of his grace, the decision has already been made for us. We now get the honor of living it out.

Schema: A Mental Map and Model for Respect

Now, here is a word that, when used, will inevitably make you look smart at parties: *schema*. The word was introduced by Swiss developmental psychologist Jean Piaget in 1923. Piaget is known for being among the most influential figures contributing to an understanding of children's thinking. He believed that children are "inventive explorers" (that is, constructivists) who are constantly constructing schemes to represent what they know and are modifying these cognitive structures through the processes of organization and adaptation.[5] So, schema is simply a mental map and model, or how we organize information regarding certain information and relationships.

One of my all-time favorite movies is Pixar's *Inside Out*. In the movie, Riley is an eleven-year-old girl living in Minnesota and loving life until her father gets a new job in San Francisco, and they have to move. The transition of moving is told from the perspective of Riley's five emotions: Joy, Sadness, Fear, Disgust, and Anger. These personified emotions help navigate Riley through all the ups and downs of moving to a new city, going to a new school, and missing all the familiarities of her old life. The emotions seek to accomplish this by keeping Riley's islands of personality healthy. There were five islands: Family Island, Honesty Island, Hockey Island, Friendship Island, and Goofball Island.

Riley's islands of personality were her schema. As a person grows, there is more and more information and experiences to process, and this is how the brain compartmentalizes. That is why it is better to think of our minds as picture galleries rather than Excel spreadsheets. If you think about it for a while, you can probably begin to imagine your islands of personality.

There is perhaps Family Island, School or Work Island, maybe College Football Island (okay, that one is for me), Friendship Island, and on and on it goes.

With all that in mind (no pun intended), the concept of respect is so important there needs to be a mental map and model for it. Just like Riley had an Honesty Island, we need a Respect or Reputation Island. The following are seven areas that make up a mental map and model for respect.

Personhood: "Honor Everyone"

The often-quoted Theodor Seuss Geisel (Dr. Seuss) wrote and illustrated forty-four books, forever changing the face of children's literature. One of my favorites is *Horton Hears a Who!* In the book, the main character is Horton the elephant, who can hear the Whos that live in Whoville, a small planet attached to a piece of dust. He is the only one who can listen to them and is mocked by all the other animals for his seemingly crazy cause. But Horton was courageous and remained resolute in his protection of Whoville, saying, "A person's a person, no matter how small!"

The best life ever lived is one devoted to valuing the lives of others. We care deeply and choose to honor people because they are . . . well . . . people. If a person is a person, they are made in God's image and worth honoring. Understanding God as the author of human life motivates the follower of Jesus to respect all persons. We are taught in the Scriptures to "Honor everyone. Love the brothers and sisters. Fear God. Honor the emperor" (1 Pet. 2:17).

There are four instructions in this one verse. First, show honor to everyone. At the time Peter wrote these words, there were 60,000,000 slaves in the Roman Empire. And each slave was by law, not a person, but a thing, with no rights whatsoever.[6] A person is never a tool, a thing, a means to an end, but rather the only creature stamped with the thumbprint of God.

The second is to love our brothers and sisters in Christ. The third to reserve the highest reverence for God himself, who is the king of the universe. The fourth is to honor the governing authorities of the land. In all four cases, the idea is to *keep and love now and in the future.*

James, the brother of Jesus, wrote what has been called "a wonderful companion piece to the teachings of Jesus as recorded in the four Gospels."[7] He dedicates a significant amount of space to the idea of showing respect to everyone:

> Do not show favoritism as you hold on to the faith in our glorious Lord Jesus Christ. For if someone comes into your meeting wearing a gold ring and dressed in fine clothes, and a poor person dressed in filthy clothes also comes in, if you look with favor on the one wearing the fine clothes and say, "Sit here in a good place," and yet you say to the poor person, "Stand over there," or "Sit here on the floor by my footstool," haven't you made distinctions among yourselves and become judges with evil thoughts?
>
> Listen, my dear brothers and sisters: Didn't God choose the poor in this world to be rich in faith and heirs of the kingdom that he has promised to those who love him? Yet you have dishonored the poor. Don't the rich oppress you and drag you into court?

Don't they blaspheme the good name that was
invoked over you?

Indeed, if you fulfill the royal law prescribed in the Scripture, Love your neighbor
as yourself, you are doing well. If, however,
you show favoritism, you commit sin. (James
2:1–9)

I can't help but wonder if James thought about his brother's teaching on humility in Luke 14:7–14. It was here that
Jesus taught that we should avoid self-exaltation, which is a
form of pride often wrapped in insecurity.

In any case, to show respect by honoring only certain
people stands in contradiction to the statement: "Honor everyone" (1 Pet. 2:17). James is teaching us about discrimination.
The example he uses has an exciting irony to it. The tendency
seems to be that some showed favoritism based on someone's
appearance. To the best, goes the best seat in the house. To
those who were undesirables . . . well, you may get a seat on
the floor. And yet, not one person who has ever been redeemed
deserved the best seat in the house. Jesus dined with sinners
during his earthly ministry because sinners are precisely the
audience he came to save. In other words, Jesus was a magnet
for the undesirables who were often overlooked by an upper-
class crowd. But that is what is so amazing about grace: Jesus
desired the undeserving. And through the person and work
of Christ, the sinner gets the best seat in the house. The best
place to sit, the position of honor, was next to the host at a
Jewish banquet. We each hold a place of honor because we are
sons and daughters of King Jesus. Our honor is based on Jesus
adopting us into his family.

It's like when we were all in grade school, and the recess bell would ring. Everyone would go to the playground to play basketball or kickball, or some other game. Captains were designated, and then the grueling process of choosing teams would commence. Of course, the captains chose the coolest or most athletic kids first. The rest of us tried not to appear anxious with each passing moment our name was not spoken.

The grace of Jesus is that he stepped onto the playgrounds of each of our lives and said, "I choose you first." We show honor because we have been chosen and set apart to the gospel of God.

We are offered a severe warning of becoming "judges with evil thoughts" (James 2:4). God has not called us to sit on high, giving us the perfect angle to look down our noses in the judgment of someone. Instead, he calls us to be servants by choosing to respect by honoring whoever the near ones might be. When we do this, we "fulfill the royal law prescribed in Scripture" (v. 8). After all, there is only one royal Lawgiver, only one judge of the universe, and he is forever merciful and just.

So let's honor everyone, no matter how much money they have or don't have in a bank account or how many followers they have or don't have on social media, no matter their sexual orientation, ethnicity, religion, societal status, or political convictions. Care for those who have everything and feel empty and those who are less fortunate and feel abandoned. Value believing partiality is a sin and that you can't show favoritism and love well simultaneously. Esteem all because you are a person that has already decided to respect all by showing honor to all.

Motivations: When Motive Is Right, Belief in Others Is Healthy

There is a centralized cause, something that drives a person deep from the inside. There is a force that is the reason for our actions. You can't look at it through a microscope or extract it from someone's DNA. Its essence is immaterial. In Victor Hugo's masterpiece *Les Misérables*, Cosette says, "A man is not idle because he is absorbed in thought. There is a visible labor and invisible labor."[8] Motivation is the invisible labor that serves as our inner cause to live, think, and love in a certain way. Make no mistake about it: a person's motivation will be a mighty force for good or evil. Everyone is motivated by something—even Jesus.

An incredible conversation happened at a well outside of a town in Samaria between Jesus and a Samaritan woman with a widespread reputation for immorality. The discussion was just between the two of them while the disciples were off gathering supplies and food. When the disciples returned to Jesus, they insisted that he eat something and give his weary body some nourishment. He refused to eat, which confused the disciples all the more. Maybe someone brought him some food already. They began to discuss among themselves. Just then, Jesus interjected: "My food is to do the will of him who sent me and to finish his work" (John 4:34).

Jesus' purpose was to do the Father's work and redeem people. His mission nourished him. As the late Eugene Peterson wrote in *The Message*: "The Word became flesh and blood, and moved into the neighborhood" (John 1:14 MSG). Jesus moved into humanity's neighborhood to make it possible for humanity to move back into God's neighborhood. It was this mission that nurtured and sustained his soul to continue onward until the work was completed. Jesus was motivated by the mission.

Because Jesus was motivated by the mission, we should then be motivated by the mesmerizing idea that we were the intended benefactor of God's mission. And so our motivation, the invisible labor of our lives and that which nourishes our soul, should be wholly different. We should be exhaustively motivated by *for God so loved . . . ME*! If I am motivated by the love of Jesus, that love causes me to respect and honor others' motivations.

Respecting the inner cause, the driving force in someone else, is a road less traveled in a culture that thrives on gotcha news and cancelling voices. But what a beautiful way to live, believing the best about someone else. To believe the best about someone, refusing judgment on people's motivation, is so countercultural that it might confuse. People have a hard time understanding someone who doesn't fit into typical boxes. I guess it is because there is often an assumption made about those who refuse to pass judgment or be critical. The assumption goes something like this: *Well, if she or he isn't against them, they must be for them.*

But what if that is the point?

What if those who follow Jesus refuse to be against anyone?

Now, don't write me off just yet. Just consider this: What if we had such confidence in the person and work of Jesus that we didn't feel the need to run around acting like the Bible police? You see, being for someone doesn't mean you agree with that person; it just means you don't see them as an enemy, but rather someone worth honoring. Believing in the authenticity of someone's motivations implies that you have chosen love and kindness, and it is the kindness of God that leads people to change. Sure, there are plenty of people with horrible and dark motivations. And yes, we will inevitably get deceived when that person chooses to do something hurtful. Even still, I would rather be deceived doing the right thing than live with a sinful skepticism that prevents me from loving well. If someone turns out to have wrong motivations, and it hurts you, remember that you are in good company. We can still look like Jesus when believing the best about someone and being wronged.

Talent: The Joyful Ability to Esteem Others' Abilities

Every person has been given a talent or talents. We all can do something well. Now ask yourself: From where did those abilities come? The Creator of all life, in his wisdom, created each of us with certain skills and abilities. And these gifts from God are intended to be used in service to others. Our responsibility is to recognize and cultivate the various skills and talents that God has given to us.

My mother spent nearly forty years working in almost every area of nursing the field offers. She concluded her career managing the nurses for a large hospital in Colorado. She had some mad skills that enabled her to pursue her profession with a standard of excellence that caused her to be a trusted ally to some of the best surgeons and hospitals in our country. That was what she was paid to do for her first career. Year in and year out, she was always drawn to the arts but rarely had the luxury of time to pursue it. While she has decided not to make a career out of it, she is now in full artistic mode. Each time I see her, she has painted something new or taken a class to grow in her ability to paint utilizing a specific technique. It is incredible to see. She sits down with a handful of brushes, watercolors, a canvas with some blue tape holding it secure, and a glass of water with a paper towel next to it. With these few tools at her disposal, she can fill the canvas with beautiful scenes from the picture gallery in her mind. My wife and I have her artwork in almost every room in our house.

I can't paint. And I would pass out after five minutes in a room where surgery was taking place. There is a lot I can't do and, spoiler alert, there are many skills that many of us lack. Yet so many focus so much time on the talents they don't have that they neglect to see how God has gifted them. It is a preposterous waste of time to be consumed with the skills we wish we had. Stop looking around at others and look in the mirror. Stop the disappointment and discover the capacity that has been granted. Find it, cultivate it, and use it to make much of Jesus. Serve this way so that some "may see your good works and give glory to your Father in heaven" (Matt. 5:16).

Living a life of respect means we esteem the gifts and abilities that God has given to others. We celebrate them. You see, the more skills and talent, the more capacity to point the world to the giver of good gifts. We are also not supposed to feel threatened by those who have similar talents to our own. You can tell a lot about a person by how they act around people with the same gift sets as their own. God didn't create people with similar gifts so that they may be threatened by each other.

This is a bit of a hard message for us Westerners to wrap our minds around. Typically, we see ourselves in a never-ending roller-coaster ride of competing. After all, we live in a capitalistic society, and capitalism breeds a competitive culture. And while there is some measure of competition embedded into our culture and society, a sense of competition should never detract from our respect for others' abilities. Respect for other people's abilities, whether they are competitors or not, is something for which we should be known. When we kick "feeling threatened" to the curb and honor someone's talent, it positions us to be a healthier person. It helps us maintain a life free from the clutter of useless emotions and continue to live with a sacred simplicity. After all, a redeemed person is far better suited for celebration and honor than skepticism and worry.

Role: Understanding the Value of All Contributions

Just as we have all been given talents, we fulfill a variety of roles within culture. On any given day, our paths cross with individuals contributing to our society in many ways. For example, on my way to the Student Leadership University (SLU) office, I will stop and get a coffee, pay a toll booth attendant, and say hello to the security guard as I wait for the elevator to take me to my floor. Then I get off the elevator, and in a few short steps, open our office door. Once inside, I say hello to Jeff, who runs our tours and student pastor conferences, and check in with Emily, who oversees the SLU programs; Anna, who coordinates programs and takes care of my administrative needs; Meghan, who also coordinates programs. If my count is correct, I interact with seven people from when I leave my house to the moment I sit in our conference room to do some work, (I don't have an office for my own quirky reasons.) Each person has a different job, each responsibility just as crucial as the next, all to help our society function.

I have had more jobs in my lifetime than the average person would believe. To name a few, I was a security guard at a juvenile delinquent facility, a custodian for a church, worked at a lumberyard, delivered paper, sharpened teeth for a stump grinder, stripped and cleaned floors in service stations, washed dishes, cooked, did landscaping, was a valet at a nice restaurant, and the list goes on and on. I've worked alongside all kinds of people. Some of the finest people I had the privilege of working alongside were those on work-release from a prison sentence. They were so grateful to reengage with society and so proud of a steady job.

At present, I have a much different job. On any given week, chances are that I am preaching or teaching somewhere. Some events are large, with thousands of people in attendance, and others provide a more intimate setting where ideas are discussed on a much deeper level. On the days when I am traveling, my wife is at home doing homeschool with six kids, making sure they eat their vegetables and take a bath before bedtime. Seriously, what she pulls off is monumental, to say the least.

When you are a respecter of the roles that people fulfill in society, then you know that whether it is preaching to 2,500 students, putting six kids to bed, or the man just out of prison now spending his days loading lumber into a truck, no one job is more important than the other. All vocations exist on a level playing field at the foot of the cross. Those living their best life honor the contributions of others to culture. Indeed, we live in a world that platforms some roles over others. For an example, look at how entertainers receive something akin to hero-worship. CEOs of successful companies and the creators of giant tech platforms like Facebook and Twitter and so on are revered.

But we are different because we don't have to carry the baggage of deciding who and what roles to value as more important and others as a supporting cast. There is a freedom associated with this approach to life. You see, we value all roles because we honor everyone.

Possessions

People come by property, possessions, and money in a variety of ways. Some inherit it, others marry someone with lots of money, and some work hard and catch a few lucky breaks along the way. The truth is that some people simply will have more money, property, and possessions than others. The Bible teaches us that material blessings are a blessing from God: "Happy is the person who fears the LORD, taking great delight in his commands. . . . Wealth and riches are in his house, and his righteousness endures forever" (Ps. 112:1, 3). But at the same time, there are strong warnings for those with wealth: "Instruct those who are rich in the present age not to be arrogant or to set their hope on the uncertainty of wealth, but on God, who richly provides us with all things to enjoy" (1 Tim. 6:17).

It amazes me how people with so much are so envied when Jesus clearly taught that wealthy people have immense challenges: "How hard it is for those who have wealth to enter the kingdom of God!" (Mark 10:23). Jesus then uses hyperbole to emphasize his point: "It is easier for a camel to go through the eye of a needle than for a rich person to enter the kingdom of God" (v. 25).

There is a significant danger for someone who has riches. They must guard their hearts against arrogance and an inordinate affection to strong for this world. They must always remember *if it can be earned and built with human hands, then it is not our heavenly home.* Wealth is a blessing and a terrible privilege. It must be seen as an opportunity to be generous and do good.

If you are reading this and are of some means and wealth, don't feel guilty or ashamed; instead, see it for the opportunity it is, and steward that opportunity well. And if you are reading this and do not have what would be considered wealth and riches in the present age, then honor those who do with your prayers. Pray that their hearts would remain compassionate, and they would live being known for doing good and being generous.

Relationship: From Tribal Noise and Chaos to Individual Calm and Compassion

There is a cancer-like phenomenon that has occurred right in front of our very eyes, without most of us realizing it. It is the tribalism of perspectives, driven by social media, creating a dogmatism that leaves no room for civility. In the docudrama (documentary drama) *The Social Dilemma*, a careful examination is painted of unintended causes and negative impacts of all things social media has on society. The film primarily features tech insiders, many from Silicon Valley, who left the industry for ethical reasons. Through the insight of those who helped shape the industry, we understand why social media is so addicting, how the technology and algorithms feed and then persuade the masses, and how data has become the most valuable product available in a capitalistic society. One of the more fascinating parts of the docudrama was how social media contributes significantly to a growing divide between persons within a culture.

People living in the same city can be logging onto the same social platforms, but are being fed entirely different messages from a particular perspective. It's like when Alice fell down the rabbit hole in *Alice and Wonderland*, except in this hole, you never stop falling. It is a never-ending cycle of reinforcing and deepening an individual's perspective, or what one has come to believe is their perspective. One of the more tragic aspects of this is polarization. Those who don't hold "your perspective" get continually painted through the content to be the villains standing in the way of how our culture should be. This is how citizens become enemies rather than comrades. One of the brilliant architects, when interviewed, stated: "Social media is a marketplace that trades exclusively in human futures."

I don't think anyone would argue the point that we have become more polarized in recent years. More tribal, and not in a good way. Tribal in the way that says, "My tribe is right, and yours is evil and should not be tolerated." People rarely talk anymore; they hold signs and shout at each other, cancel or shame each other. They hind on social media, trolling and commenting under a fake identity so they can spout their cowardly perspective. For all the good accomplished by social media, it doesn't seem to have made us more understanding, patient, or kind. But rather, it has made us militant in our views, quick to tear someone down, and be anything but kind.

But what if, amid all the noise and chaos, there was a calm group of people who refuse to dehumanize? Could we be a people respective of perspectives and, in turn, respectful of each other's relationships? What if we engaged with a sacred simplicity that was honorable? We could be asking questions and listening, really listening, to the answers; learning stories of those from differing tribes, while respecting both and always caring about the story right in front of us. I often wonder if people could divorce themselves from technology that indoctrinated them and just did life with someone else, if maybe they might see "others" differently. This is how we begin the journey down the road of respect—one person, one story at a time. This is how we go from tribal noise and chaos to individual calm and compassion.

Authority: Render unto Caesar

Civil discourse among governing authorities seems to have gone away and, with it, an attitude of respect for those in governing positions. This is a subjective observation from someone who struggles to have the right perspective concerning our leaders. Jesus teaches us that such struggles should also go away. Well, that is my interpretation of it. In other words, while there may, at times, be a level of impatience and frustration with governing authorities, there is never an excuse for disrespect.

There is a fascinating event that happens in Jesus' ministry. In one of their schemes to dishonor and discredit Jesus, the Pharisees asked a politically impossible question about whether or not it is lawful to pay taxes to Caesar. It doesn't seem like a big dilemma for a Western mind who enjoys the benefits of paying taxes to governing authorities (i.e., roads, military, education, etc.). But for the Jewish mind, the tension was much different since they lived under the boot-authority of the Roman Empire. In this sense, the Jews were not a free people. So, if Jesus approved of paying taxes, it would seem he supported the Roman occupation. But on the other hand, if he disapproved, it could be viewed as a treasonous act against Rome.[9]

Jesus knew this was a trap. Therefore, the Master answered masterfully, showing how to respect governing authority while demonstrating complete allegiance to God. He simply asked to see the coin, asked whose inscription was on it, and when the answer returned, "Caesar's," he said, "Give to Caesar the things that are Caesar's, and to God the things that are God's." To those who sought to entangle our Lord, they simply stood silent and amazed before taking their leave.

Now, here is where the Greek language gives us great insight into what Jesus meant. Those who questioned Jesus used a Greek word that simply meant "to give." In his response, Jesus used a different word than just "give." Instead, he used a word that speaks "to paying something as a debt."[10] You see, taxes were symbolic of submitting to the governing authorities. But why? The apostle Paul would answer this question for us when he wrote: "Let everyone submit to the governing authorities, since there is no authority except from God, and the authorities that exist are instituted by God" (Rom. 13:1). As one leader of the early church wrote a few hundred years later: "it is possible both to fulfill to men their claims and to give unto God the things that are due to God from us."[11]

The apostle Paul would also teach that, by paying taxes, we give "respect to those you owe respect, and honor to those you owe honor" (v. 7).

We are dual citizens. Ultimately, our citizenship and allegiance are to heaven and God. But in our journey through life, we are also earthly citizens who exist under governing authorities, which exist under God's sovereign control. And as we journey, God doesn't want us to carry a type of debt that can be accumulated through disrespect. Citizens are drowning in this type of debt because of a condescending attitude or cutting corners with governing authorities. Choose to live debt-free because you honored the authority, despite the politics of it all. God is not calling us to blind obedience, but to be a good and respectful citizens. In other words, dishonoring governing authorities needs to go the way of the dodo bird—extinct.

What a peaceful feeling it must be to have disrespect and dishonor become extinct in one's life.

Restitution: How to Right the Wrongs of Disrespect?

It is a rare gem that radiates with beauty when a person is willing to do whatever it takes to heal the wounds created by disrespect and dishonor. And while Zacchaeus is known throughout history for being vertically challenged, his response to the grace of Jesus makes his story powerful. Zacchaeus had the one job that would make him rich while simultaneously being the most hated man in town. As a Jew, he collected taxes on behalf of Rome, and whatever he collected over the required amount, he was allowed to pocket. This is why so many Jewish people thought of tax collectors as traitors and extortionists. It is also why tax collectors didn't walk through a crowd, because someone might pull a knife. Zacchaeus didn't just climb the sycamore tree because he was short.

Out of all the people in Jericho, Jesus chose to stay with the most notorious sinner in the region. In addition to the rumor mill running overtime, Zacchaeus's heart was warmed by the kindness of the Savior. His response to Jesus was definitive: "Look, I'll give half of my possessions to the poor, Lord. And if I have extorted anything from anyone, I'll pay back four times as much" (Luke 19:8). First, he begins with a commitment to give half of all his possessions to those in need.

This is simply evidence that a changed heart will change other people's lives.

Then he makes a curious commitment to pay back four times as much as the amount he cheated his fellow citizens. The Scottish theologian William Barclay explained the reason for such an exuberant amount of money to be repaid:

> In his restitution, he went far beyond what was legally necessary. Only if robbery was a deliberate and violent act of destruction was a fourfold restitution necessary (Exodus 22:1). If it had been an ordinary robbery and the original goods were not restorable, double the value had to be repaid (Exodus 22:4, 7). If voluntary confession was made and voluntary restitution offered, the original goods' value had to be paid, plus one-fifth (Leviticus 6:5; Numbers 5:7). Zacchaeus was determined to do far more than the law demanded. He showed by his deeds that he was a changed man.[12]

Zacchaeus had experienced the grace of Jesus. God's grace creates such a deep well of gratitude in our lives that the minimum requirement is never sufficient to right a wrong. Love leads us to do all we can to amend all our wrongs. Zacchaeus sought the kind of restitution that would possibly lead to interpersonal restoration.

So, what does our wee little friend teach us about righting wrongs thousands of years later? The word *restitution* simply means an act of restoring or a condition of being restored. Jesus-honoring restitution begins with an attitude that determines the appropriate action. This is why there isn't a one-size-fits-all plan that can be given and implemented. There are no, "Step one is . . . , step two . . . , step three . . . , and so on." Unless those steps are:

1. I have experienced the immeasurable grace of Jesus.
2. I have disrespected or dishonored a person, group, or earthly authority, and believe this is sin.
3. As a follower of Jesus, I am brokenhearted over my sin, and my attitude will be to take whatever steps are necessary to seek forgiveness.
4. Because of a "whatever it takes" attitude, my outward actions will be natural evidence of my heart and mind's condition.

I know what some of us are wondering: *But are there limits? What if I do all that I can, and forgiveness isn't reciprocated?* Interestingly, Zacchaeus's story is one in which we don't know from Scripture how those he had wronged responded.

Let us simply resolve to do all that we can. Our Lord was willing to suffer an agonizing death on the cross with the weight of the sins of the world upon his shoulders. The extent of his sacrifice to make restitution for our sin so that a relationship with God could be restored . . . seems to be beyond the limits of human comprehension. Following Jesus' example, we should do all that we can, love well in light of our wrongs, and keep on loving because we have experienced forgiveness. May we seek to love in light of our shortcomings and to keep on loving until the song of redemption drowns out the sin of disrespect.

An exercise in imagination.

Imagine a society where people respected each other all the time; where wrongs were righted, and what was lost became restored; where people who had been dishonored were valued and celebrated beyond the minimum requirement. What a society it would be if persons in it were known for restorative action. Imagine what a world it could be.

Maybe that's too broad . . .

What would happen if those who have had the song of God's saving grace sung over their lives decided to sing forth a loving response to wrongs that need to be righted? What if, in singing the song of God's restorative love, a person became someone that sees the infinite value in people who have been dishonored? People make up the church. So what if these people, these churches, decided to spend their time caring and honoring everyone? What beautiful culture they could create in the communities where they lived and loved. Maybe, just maybe, this culture could look a little bit like heaven. And what if we spent so much time respecting and honoring in this culture that people began to think: *I want to sing that song too*?

9

Integrity

Step 9: Shine like Stars in the World

Valeting Cars and the Night Character Died

I had recently fallen in love with Christina. She is the incredible women I mentioned in the chapter on relationships. I knew within one week that I would spend all the other weeks of my life loving her and her alone. We lived several states apart, and at the age of twenty-two, I was serving with an awesome ministry where my role required raising one's own funds for support. Needless to say, I was strapped for cash big-time. Fundraising wasn't working out very well so I got a job valeting cars at a nice restaurant in the evenings. When I wasn't out on the road serving alongside this incredible ministry, I would serve in their offices from 9:00 to 4:30 each day. At which point, I would drive to the restaurant, park in the back of the parking lot, climb into the back seat, and change clothes. Why didn't I change before leaving the office? Honestly, I didn't want anyone to know I couldn't raise the money through donations to work with this ministry, so I got a night job.

So there I would be, parking cars night after night until midnight or 1:00 in the morning. The tips I made valeting cars allowed me to rent a small room in a house, which was more than enough space. At this point in life, I had a mattress, a handful of books, and enough clothes to fill one drawer. Oh, and I knew God wanted me to marry Christina and spend the rest of my life sharing the good news of Jesus.

Now, I wanted to buy my future wife the engagement ring she deserved. We actually went and looked at rings together. Knowing my financial situation, she picked out the cheapest ring in the store and then acted like it was the most amazing thing she had ever seen. Honestly, she could have won an Oscar with her performance that day. And she would have worn it with great joy the rest of her life because she is simply that special breed of woman who places more value in joy and laughter than fancy things. Nonetheless, I had something much grander in mind that I knew she would love. I made a plan based on an average night's tips, mapped out how long it would take me to save the money, then set a date for when I would bend a knee.

The nights came and went. I counted and measured my progress with hopeful anticipation. The closer I got to my goal, the more happiness filled my heart. It was not because of the ring's cost, but because I genuinely felt I was giving her a ring that she truly deserved. I will never forget when I was within one week of having enough money when the unexpected happened.

The valet gig was a two-person job. We would park cars and simply run past each other all night long, parking and retrieving. At the end of the night, we called it even and split the tips. Then came the night I'll never forget. I showed up to work as usual, and the storm clouds were already brewing. This meant it was going to be an exceptionally profitable night. On nights when it rained, we typically made double tips. There was just one problem: the other guy never showed. What would be an excellent night for tips was looking like a disaster waiting to happen. People don't typically tip when they are mad because they had to wait too long for their vehicle.

Such is life. By 6:00 p.m., the cars were lined up and down the street. I was running and parking and handing tickets as fast as I possibly could. The harder I worked, the longer the line seemed to grow. I was soaked to the bone, giving it all I had, and making progress at a snail-like pace.

By around 7:30 p.m., I had everything under control as the dinner-rush wave subsided. From that moment on, it was soggy shoes and managing the steady-but-not-frantic flow of incoming customers. Sometime after 8:00 p.m., an SUV pulled up with two college-age ladies in the front seats and what appeared to be their two guys who were their dates in the back seats. I walked over to the driver's door, opened it, and welcomed her to the restaurant. I must have been quite a sight to her! I had been sprinting in a thunderstorm for two hours, and there was no amount of politeness that could hide wet clothes hanging off my skinny frame and water still dripping off my damp head. *The one night I didn't bring a towel!* I thought to myself. Meanwhile, the kind lady said, "Looks like you have had a pretty rough night. I hope this helps." She put a five-dollar bill in my hand. I replied, "Thank you! I am fine, and I hope you and your friends have a great meal."

I then proceeded to park her car in the section blocked off for valet services. It was still thundering and lightning like it was the end times. I parked her vehicle, got out, and proceeded to put the key in the door to lock it. I guess because of the storm, I wasn't paying much attention and the next thing I know, I had put the wrong key in the door and broke it off.

I went back to my station and resolved to myself that I would just have to confess as soon as they exited the restaurant. Akin to ripping off a Band-Aid, I would say, "Ma'am, I am so sorry, but I put the wrong key in your door lock and broke it off. Whatever the cost, I will pay to have it fixed." As I rehearsed the different ways the scene could unfold in my mind, and after some time had passed, the two couples emerged from their nice meal. I pulled her vehicle around and decided that I would find the courage and tell her as soon as I could get out of the car. When I stepped out of the car, she was standing there with another five-dollar tip. She placed it in my hand and said with a kind smile, "I hope your night has gotten better."

I looked at the second five-dollar bill in my hand, looked back at her, and said, "Thank you, and I hope you guys have a great rest of your evening." They drove away, and sometime later, I went home.

That night I went to the little room I rented, sat down on the floor next to my single mattress, and counted my tips. That night it was all one-dollar bills in one stack and two five-dollar bills alone in another. It was like my lie was staring me back in the face saying: "Is your integrity worth ten dollars?" I didn't sleep that night and, honestly, I didn't repent of my sin either. I lay in bed staring at the ceiling, thinking about all the good I was doing working for an evangelistic nonprofit, raising my own support, trying to marry a godly woman, and on and on it went.

The next day was a blur. I navigated my nonprofit job in a zombie-like state and found myself back in my trying-to-make-a-profit job valeting cars that evening. Early in my shift, the manager came out and said, "I received an unusual call today. A woman valeted her car here last night and said someone broke off a key to her office in the driver's side door. She said they went to a couple of clubs after the restaurant where they valeted the vehicle so it could have happened there. I assured her that you weren't that kind of guy, but I would ask anyway. Know anything about it?"

I lied again.

That night I went home and counted my tips. I felt dead inside. I mean, I am a Christian, and I lied twice over a few bucks. Sometime after midnight in the fall of 2001, I broke down in a way that had never happened before. I cried. No, I wept. Looking at that money, I saw what the old preachers referred to as *the sinfulness of my sin*. I repented. I repented again. I just kept telling Jesus how sorry I was. And I committed that night: No matter the cost, I would never cover up a mistake with a lie. I promised Jesus that night that I would never lie again. I know that may seem unrealistic, but a broken heart makes bold promises, promises that are commitments.

I did everything I could to confess to anyone who I had wronged. And, though I make a ton of mistakes, I have never lost sight of the promise I made to God that night. My goal has been to avoid the darkness, shine the light, and live free. If I've learned anything about seeking after one's best life, it involves freedom of the soul that can only come from living in the light.

Devils among Us: Recognizing Shade in a Shady World

The world is shady and growing shadier still. There are devils among us, and every time we choose a lie over the truth, we act as devils. It is so easy to see the devil at work in the world around us, and it is exponentially more difficult to see him staring back in the mirror, especially when it's the rear-view mirror in someone's car you are parking. If we are ever to live our best lives, we must be committed to walking in the light of truth every day, in every conversation, with every post on social media, and every use of our resources.

Let's begin with a clear understanding: all falsehood, all lies, find their source in the enemy, the devil himself. Satan is the enemy that seeks to deceive so that we may stay dead to the truth and goodness of Jesus. In one of the strongest statements in the Bible regarding Satan's personality, Jesus said:

> "Why don't you understand what I say? Because you cannot listen to my word. You are of your father the devil, and you want to carry out your father's desires. He was a murderer from the beginning and does not stand in the truth, because there is no truth in him. When he tells a lie, he speaks from his own nature, because he is a liar and the father of lies. Yet because I tell the truth, you do not believe me." (John 8:43–45)

To personally know Jesus is to see the truth and to live. To *not* know Jesus leaves us with the option of being part of a terrible tribe, one that only knows death. The enemy does not love, and there isn't an ounce of compassion in his being. He is the most selfish creature ever to exist. He wants only death and destruction. His evil desires are a reflection of his monstrous appetite for deceit and murder; it is an appetite that can never be satisfied. So, based on Jesus' description of the devil, we can conclude that a lie is any form of communication that is designed and meant to deceive.

On a very practical level, what does deceit look like in our current world? Study after study echoes what most of us already feel and know: trust is eroding. We trust each other less and many believe that the downward trend in trusting government makes it even harder to solve societal problems.[1] Though lying is as old as time itself, humanity seems to find more creative ways to platform this deceit with each passing chapter of history. There is nothing new under the sun, including lying, but depraved people will always find ways to express their depravity.

Remember, most of us think that the big bad liars of the world are out there, roaming the streets of Babylon, wearing their deception like a team jersey. This is rarely the case. Lying is among us and is something that most people will struggle with on one level or another. But why do we lie? The types of lies we tell speak to the "why" for our falsehoods. Here are five types of lies that can serve as categories to summarize the landscape of active deception:

1. The Malicious Lie: *violating the truth to deceive and, thus, hurt someone*

Example

Question: "Do you know who started that awful rumor about me having an eating disorder?"

Lie: "No idea, that is terrible!"

This is one of the most evident types of lies to identify. It is a malicious and wicked attempt to tear down someone's reputation by constructing or contributing to a message that violates the truth.

2. The Insecure Lie: *allowing fear to prevent transparency and determine a falsehood conveyed*

Example

Question: "How are you doing today?"

Lie: "I'm fine," or, "I'm doing well. How about you?"

This is one of the most common lies told. This type of duplicity is often a two-way street because both the person asking and the person answering are deceitful. We ask about someone's well-being without really wanting a transparent answer, and we answer such questions without a willingness to be transparently honest. It is a common courtesy that is one of the most common lies.

3. The Prideful Lie: *an arrogant attempt to cover up weaknesses or wrongs*

Example

"I am so glad that you two have decided to go through premarital counseling leading up to the big day. In our meetings, we are going to discuss both your past, personalities, and how best to serve each other in the covenant relationship of marriage."

A counseling session or two later:

Question: "Have either of you struggled with looking at pornography? My reason for asking this question is because it is certainly something that neither of you wants to carry into a marriage."

Lie: "I saw a few images when I was in middle and high school, but I do not look at pornography."

Prideful lies destroy more relationships than any other kind. It is the height of arrogance to believe that we are strong enough to solve all of our problems in a vacuum. A prideful lie's end goal is always to save face and appear to be in complete control. This lie denies the fundamental need we have for each other: "confess your sins to one another and pray for one another, so that you may be healed. The prayer of a righteous person is very powerful in its effect" (James 5:16).

4. The Personal Advantage Lie: *repositioning my story to make it appear more appealing*

Example

Question: "I follow you on social media. How do you manage to meet so many interesting people and have so many unique experiences?"

Lie: "Well, the Lord has really blessed me, and I just grab a pic here and there to let people know what is going on."

These are lies that focus on exaggeration, brand association, and staging everything that appears publicly to reinforce the desired story line. By exaggeration, we mean that it is easier to say you caught a fish nearly 10 pounds than one that weighed 8.25 pounds, or by seeking to gain influence and acceptance through a false perception of association with people who have achieved success. In the end, this is the type of lie where one manipulates the communication to portray a false narrative that will lead to opportunities and benefits.

5. The Convenient Lie: *choosing the ease of duplicity to facilitate a more comfortable existence*

Example

Question: "Are you able to meet up with our small group tonight?"

Lie: "No, I'm not feeling well."

Question: "Hey, the movie starts in fifteen minutes. What time will you guys get here?"

Lie: "Traffic is crazy bad, and my girlfriend was running a little late because her mom needed her to stop by the pharmacy to pick up her prescription."

These types of lies usually have two ingredients. First, it helps us feel better about something rather than just being honest. Second, it shifts blame to circumstances outside of our control: health, traffic, someone else's needs. This lie masks itself as outwardly and others focused, but it is selfish and cowardly in reality.

Most lying in this shady world will occur under one of the five above categories. And it is important to see each lie for what it is so that we can position our lives to never carry such baggage. Each lie is a deception that we have to take with us. As time goes by, the weight of it all grows and grows. Our best life can never be discovered in the shadows; it cannot be found under the heavy load of lies accumulated. We were meant to travel light, and we were told to travel in the light. Life is most enjoyed when we don't have to look over our shoulders, and when we can keep our focus on what is ahead. In the end, we must live with the understanding that we have only one enemy, and we are enemies of his ways.

Catching Light: "Shine like Stars in the World"

One of the reasons we left living in a subdivision, right outside a major city, is so we could look at the stars at night. I know that sounds odd, but hear me out. Living so close to everything made it hard to have an undiluted view of the night sky. And on the rare nights that one could see the stars clearly, there was always the noise of traffic and airplanes and sirens and neighbors and on and on. We loved where we lived, but we wanted a change.

An hour outside of the city and down a little dirt road changed my view. Now, I walk outside every night and look up into the vastness of space while observing God's glory on tour in the sky. The stars shine brighter in the country. And the soundtrack of the wind blowing through the trees, the old barn owl serenading the forest, and the bullfrogs endlessly responding to each other makes the viewing experience all the more serene. Often, I get lost in thought sitting on the back porch, looking and listening to creation. A starlit night is a thing of beauty that I hope I never take for granted.

The stars, each positioned by God's hand, appearing in the night sky are an astronomical metaphor. They symbolize the role and character of our lives in a dark and shady world. Paul would write about this when encouraging the Philippian believers to "be blameless and pure, children of God who are faultless in a crooked and perverted generation, among whom you shine like stars in the world, by holding firm to the word of life" (Phil. 2:15–16).

Shine Like Stars

What does it mean to shine like a star? Essentially, it means we are to be a contrast to the darkness around us. If we live in a shady world that is only growing shadier, we stand out as those who are catching the light. Probably a correct way of saying it is that the Light caught us. And because our lives have become illuminated by the gospel of God, we choose a more redemptive approach. Seeing the light means that we seek to accentuate the positive, the honest, and the good that exists. We refuse to play catch in a world of throwing shade. We are different. The light of Jesus motivates us to be an illuminating force in a dark world.

One scholar described light this way: "'Light' is a beautiful illustration of something that does what it has to do by being what it ought to be."[2] Jesus taught us in the Sermon on the Mount that if we are redeemed, then we are to be light. To put it bluntly, as it pertains to our character, *being people of integrity and character is simply doing what we are supposed to do because we are who we ought to be.* And this is continually accomplished by holding firm to the Word of Life. The Word of Life is simply the message that gives life, the message of Jesus. Therefore, the more we know Jesus, the closer we are to him, the better positioned we are to shine like stars in the world.

Integrity, then, allows the light in you to shine through you in word and deed. It is choosing between throwing shade and catching the light. Between slipping into the darkness or radiating the light of Jesus from within us; between somehow attempting to live a dormant and deceived lives and working out our salvation.

The story of a luminary is that she or he is of good character. Their integrity runs deep and is woven into their now unfolding narrative. They can lie or twist the truth, but choose not to because they live overwhelmed by the Truth that resides inside them. They let their light shine like stars on the dark canvas of a night sky because the Light of the world has taken up residence in their souls. They are the rare breed of persons whose "yes" means "yes," and their "no" means "no," as Jesus taught, and "anything more than this is from the evil one" (Matt. 5:37).

Integrity: *Liberavi Animam Meam*

Saint Bernard of Clairvaux is an interesting conundrum in the halls of church history. On one hand, he was an eloquent preacher and writer who earned the nickname "the honey-tongued doctor." He helped reform monasteries and founded over a hundred in his lifetime. In many ways, he was a mystic in the medieval chapter of history whose works still live on to this day. He wrote with profound clarity that, in turn, led the reader to deep reflection with such words as:

> For when God loves, all He desires is to be loved in return. The sole purpose of His love is to be loved, in the knowledge that those who love Him are made happy by their love of Him.[3]

It seems that Saint Bernard truly desired the life of a monk, living in solitude and practicing his version of spiritual discipline. But because of his eloquent speech, deep theological insight, and the number of students who had emerged from his monasteries, he was needed continuously to solve political disputes or advise popes.

While many good things could be said of the man, like most characters who darken the stage of history's theater, not all were positive. Bernard played a significant role in the Second Crusade, preaching and inspiring many to abandon their current occupation and take up the cause of Christ by going to war with the Muslim armies for control of Jerusalem. Even a casual glance at history leads us to believe the Second Crusade was unsuccessful, unnecessary, and steeped in bloodshed.

If anything, Bernard is like so many figures from Christian history: sinful leaders who sometimes did evil things but were also used to accomplish some good for followers of Jesus. This is why, even nearly a thousand years after his death, some find his writings on the love of God and loving Jesus helpful.

So why the brief history lesson on a monk from so long ago? In AD 1152, he was asked to write a letter to shed light on a certain church leader's dishonest practices. Though Bernard struggled with the task because of the danger of the letter being circulated or read aloud, out of conviction and submitting to the Catholic church's authority, he agreed. Toward the end of the letter, he wrote an amazing little Latin phrase that translates into: "I have freed my soul."[4] He was essentially saying, "I have been honest concerning a leader who was abusing his authority through deceit, and my conscience is clear."

I have freed my soul.

What a beautiful phrase. To have the soul disentangled from any form of dishonesty must be a glorious feeling. While we could also say, the most tortured soul is drowning in the shadows of deception, longing for the light so they can breathe again. Yet, the light which gives freedom is available because God "made the one who did not know sin to be sin for us, so that in him we might become the righteousness of God" (2 Cor. 5:21). Through Jesus, the righteousness of God is credited to all who have been made new creations in Christ. Jesus makes us holy. We are women and men of character and integrity who have been called out of the shadows and into the light. Jesus made it possible to breathe again for the first time since the garden of Eden.

The choice to trust what God has accomplished inside us is the faith-filled daily decision to live out the freedom given to us. Jesus has freed our souls; now, it is our responsibility to live free. This is why Jesus taught: "If you continue in my word, you really are my disciples. You will know the truth, and the truth will set you free" (John 8:31–32). It is our responsibility to "continue in" the enlightenment given to us through the words of Jesus. That is why we choose honesty in every decision and all ways, not because we are adhering to a moral code. But because we are free.

> Every day we walk in the light and breath in the new mercies of God, we can say with Saint Bernard of Clairvaux, "I have freed my soul."

> When we are confronted with opportunities where it is easier to lie . . .

> When it is simpler to exaggerate than be exact . . .

> When the slanderers are spreading their deceitfulness . . .

> And when silence is the nonconfrontational and comfortable option . . .

We can choose to walk in the light and speak and act with truth and grace. And whenever the option presents itself to slip back into the shadows, we choose to stay in the light because we have been set free. And in so doing, we have freed our souls.

I'll never forget the feeling I had when I traded my soul for a few bucks outside a nice restaurant all those years ago. It is a memory that will not be erased. It is also a memory that does not imprison me. For while my character died that night, Jesus resurrected it. Nothing is impossible with God, and that means that moments of dishonesty will not define us in his sight. Never forget that we worship a God who can make all things new. Sometimes I think God is just waiting on us to realize his goodness and how grace-filled he will be if we bring our brokenness to him. It is then we get to witness God do what only God can do—forgive us and allow us to live in his grace.

We cannot escape our lies, but we can run into the arms of a forgiving Father. We can choose to live in the light. And in so doing, make better the lives of those around us. In one sense, our integrity exists for the betterment of those around us. As we engage our family, friends, coworkers, and so forth, being people of good character improves their lives. On the other hand, if we are untrustworthy and people of little integrity, we'll hurt ourselves and those around us. So, let's live our best lives; one that doesn't throw shade because it is too busy catching the light. Let it be a life that sees the sinfulness of our sin, repents, and lives in God's forgiveness; a life that is of good and trustworthy character because we are working out our salvation. May it be a life that has been set free by the only One who would free our souls and then lives that freedom daily. And in so doing, *shine like stars in the world*.

10

Contentment

Step 10: Submit and Delight in the Desires of the Good Father

Content is the person whose happiness is achieved by finding joy and satisfaction in things that will outlive her or him. In a world where everyone is their own photojournalist, portraying a not-so-accurate view of their life, how can we stop trying to find our place in the noise? Better yet, how can we discover that incredible jewel called *contentment*?

Many of us are trying to keep up, measure up, or stand out . . . and it is exhausting. We are a society of doing more and more, hoping that we will become someone more than our present station in life. But more isn't the answer, and neither is keeping up with or measuring up to someone else. To attempt to live someone else's life is another way of replicating a life never intended to be lived by you. It only leads to unhappiness. When we are discontented, our lives become riddled with comparisons, anxiety, and worry over image and status, and unhealthy desires that contribute to a harmful condition.

All of this has nothing to do with living well. So how do we repair the despair? It is this question that leads us to the final step of discovering and living our best lives. There is a form of discontentment that is helpful and even healthy. We can be discontented with injustice and the brokenness of this world, or we can be displeased with our spiritual growth.[1] But these are not the chief aim of the following discussion. Let me state my desire for this chapter as clearly as possible: God wants you to be at peace and enjoy a contentment that can only be established through him. J. I. Packer explained that those who know God have great contentment in him: "There is no peace like the peace of those whose minds are possessed with full assurance that they have known God, and God has known them, and that this relationship guarantees God's favor to them in life, through death and on forever."[2]

It is my sincerest prayer that you would experience the peace of God . . . and be content.

Bored in Babylon

Babylon was one of the most important, affluent, and influential cities of the ancient world. Its ancient name probably meant "the gate of the gods."[3] This name biblically finds its greatest notoriety under King Nebuchadnezzar. This would be the city where young Daniel was deported after the king's vast army conquered his city. The prophet Zechariah described it as the place where wickedness made its home. It was a place of idolatry where every sinful inclination could be indulged under the banner of worship. Being the place of all the gods, Nebuchadnezzar first worshiped Marduk or Bel, who was known as the chief deity of Babylon[4] and believed to be the god of creation and destiny.[5]

Nebuchadnezzar wanted his destiny to be filled with military conquests, his temple to be filled with valuable sacred symbols from the people he conquered, his table to be filled with endless food and wine, and his throne to be served by those he had captured. Once in Babylon, Daniel and his three friends' names were changed to honor this new and foreign land's false gods. It was immediately after the name-change event that we read: "Daniel determined that he would not defile himself . . ." (Dan. 1:8).

Daniel could have easily lived out his days serving in the king's court and eating the finest food from the king's table. He could have blended in with the Babylonian culture, reveling in all the indulgences worthy of a place that was the gateway of the gods.

What a life he could have enjoyed!

There is just one problem: Daniel had already discovered the significance of his own name. His name literally meant "God is my judge." His soul had awakened to a truth that has endured for millennia: *after discovering contentment in the one true God, no other god, activity, or earthly luxury can satisfy one's soul.*

Though most of us haven't been physically captured against our will and taken to a foreign land, a Babylon-like experience is present and ever available. We live in a world that can meet every need in a moment. If we live in America or many other places around the world, our choices are endless. We get to choose whether we want to eat Thai or Italian for dinner, oh, and, have it delivered. Then, we can enjoy the evening's entertainment by streaming any show or movie we want or just watch our favorite YouTuber. During such time, we can take part in the roller-coaster ride of scrolling through images and messages on social media. We can order anything from anywhere, and most of the time, it appears on our doorsteps the next day. Yep, life can be pretty easy here in Babylon.

The problem is that for so many of us, it's never enough. What a sad place it is when the soundtrack of our lives is "never enough." As the song from the 2017 musical *The Greatest Showman* expresses it: "All the stars we steal from the night sky will never be enough."[6]

"It's never enough" is why there are so many reports about the sex-trafficking linked to a culture's consumption of pornography. "It's never enough" leads to substance abuse to numb the empty feeling in people with the world at their fingertips. "It's never enough" is why so many are chasing after a form of happiness that will never satisfy. I think it is a fair assessment to say, by and large, we are a discontented people, and through our discontented condition, we have made the world worse.

Babylon is only a problem if you see it as your home, your identity. The deeply discontented person is comfortably at home where wickedness resides. You see, Daniel was deported to Babylon, but his identity was still with the people of his homeland. That is why Babylon couldn't add to Daniel's life, but he could certainly help them. When God is enough, when the grace of Jesus is something you have experienced, then Babylon can't offer you anything close.

Many are bored in Babylon because it has become their identity; they've made a home out of a place they were never intended to dwell. Let me say it this way: we are discontented when our souls are too easily satisfied with culture's trappings rather than the God of creation. The need to feed our need to consume has led us to be bored in a culture of desiring more. A discontented person will never live their best life, and they won't contribute to a better world.

When people become bored in Babylon, it detrimentally impacts culture. The late cultural critic and educator Neil Postman wrote prophetically in his book *Amusing Ourselves to Death*: "When a population becomes distracted by the trivia, when cultural life is redefined as a perpetual round of entertainments, when serious public conversation becomes a form of baby-talk, when, in short, a people become an audience and their public business a vaudeville act, then a nation finds itself at risk; culture-death is a clear possibility."[7] By the way, Postman wrote that in 1985! A discontented people will deteriorate rapidly until all that formerly remains concerning that people . . . looks dead. Babylon should warn us that an indulged people mistake true happiness for feeding a depraved hunger.

The Fictitious Furnishing of the Fake Best Life

Let's focus in and give some categories of what we thought would be our best life, but actually contribute to a discontented state—the fictitious furnishing of our fake life. Jesus taught us clearly that "one's life is not in the abundance of his possessions" (Luke 12:15). And yet, it is so easy to fall prey to greed and furnish our lives with things that don't add anything to our lives. Greed, which can be understood as an unhealthy desire for more, is the enemy of contentment. This is why Jesus additionally taught:

"Don't store up for yourselves treasures on
earth, where moth and rust destroy and where
thieves break in and steal. But store up for
yourselves treasures in heaven, where neither
moth nor rust destroys, and where thieves
don't break in and steal. For where your treasure is, there your heart will be also." (Matt.
6:19–21)

Some very well-meaning people have believed Jesus was
teaching that his followers should not own many possessions. But this is not a rich-versus-poor, have-versus-have-nots
idea. Treasure can mean different things to different people.
Because our treasure is what we value and focus on with
our lives, treasure is what we long to possess. Some may say,
"That's easy for you to say; try being poor!" However, the
Bible teaches that it is harder for a rich person to understand
heaven's treasure.

If it's not specifically about "stuff," then what is Jesus
teaching? He is addressing the motive behind owning material
possessions. Whatever we value, whatever we possess or long
to have in this life, should be valued with the heart of heaven
in mind. This is why Jesus doesn't specifically define what is
"the treasure of heaven." Because whatever our treasure on the
earth may be, it should be cared for according to what matters to God. That is to say that we use our earthly resources
according to the priorities of God's kingdom. Therefore, an
earthly treasure isn't synonymous with heavenly glory. But
this mindset transforms what we value in the here and now,
as tools and resources, to the treasure that will live on past the
grave: character and personal holiness, obedience to the faith,

seeing people transformed by the good news of Jesus, and disciples nurtured in the faith.[8]

To be rightly motivated by our earthly resources means we are investing in eternity. We live in a measurable moment and have been allowed to invest in a place where moments will become immeasurable and go on forever. Jesus also gives us categories to help us think through to guard our hearts against living for the wrong things. He teaches that the ultimate storehouse is in heaven. It is the one place the temporal of this world cannot deteriorate that which we have trusted to God.

If we live as if Babylon is our home, we will fill it with furnishings that can be destroyed or taken. Jesus mentions moths, rust, and thieves. Moths are mentioned because wealth often consisted of expensive fabrics for clothes. Moths can eat materials like wool, leather, and silk. It contains a protein that they can digest. Rust refers to precious metals that will eventually corrode. Some metals rust faster than others, but in any case, it is an example of stuff that will ultimately lose its shine and value as it deteriorates. Finally, the thieves speak to the idea that this world's material possessions can be taken from us.

- Moths consume
- Rust corrodes
- Thieves confiscate

To live for the temporal, spend all our days consuming and accumulating, and never use these earthly treasures for something greater than a big house with lots of toys is the very picture of materialism. Materialism is loving the type of treasure that, in the end, is a curse. The best way to avoid the hard-earned valuables we possess from being consumed, corroded, or confiscated is to use them for the glory of God.

We must ask ourselves: Are we living under the authority of what we have or wish we had? Or are the affections of our heart focused on that which will live on past the grave? When our hearts are focused on heaven, our lives are content on the earth.

Que Sera, Sera: A Little Italian Goes a Long Way

Every night my Italian wife sings a little song to our children called "*Que Sera, Sera.*" It has become the lullaby of their childhood. Even though it was performed by Doris Day and won an Oscar for Best Original Song in Alfred Hitchcock's 1956 *The Man Who Knew Too Much*, to my children, it is referred to as "the Mommy song." It's a beautiful little number that deals with the narrator asking her mother questions about the future during three seasons of life: as a child, as a young adult falling in love, and as a parent. Each phase of life asks questions about which most every person wonders: Will I be rich and pretty when I grow up? When I fall in love, will the days be filled with happiness? As a parent, instead of asking the questions, she is responding to her children asking the same questions she asked as a child. The answer is the same in each case:

> Que sera, sera,
> Whatever will be, will be
> The future's not ours to see.

I like to think the two generations of mothers in that song teach their children something about contentment. We can plan and prepare, but ultimately there are three factors at play when it comes to our future: the broken world we live in, how we utilize our freedom to make choices, and the sovereignty of God. A sinful world and our freedom are not equal, by no stretch of the imagination, to the authority of an all-powerful God exercising his authority over his creation. But I am suggesting those are primary forces that impact our futures. Now, we choose to be salt and light in a broken world, we choose to make good and wise decisions, but at the end of the day, we have to trust in the authority of God.

A part of us needs to be comfortable saying "whatever will be, will be," knowing that we have trusted our lives to the good Father. Therefore, as with all things, contentment begins with a healthy understanding of God. Writing in his raw poetic style, Brennan Manning gives us a great launching off place: "The furious longing of God is beyond our wildest desires, our hope or hopelessness, our rectitude or wickedness, neither cornered by sweet talk nor gentle persuasion. It cannot be tamed, boxed, captivated, housebroken, or temple broken. It is simply and startlingly Jesus, the effulgence of the Father's love."[9] Put plainly, we can experience heaven and hell on the earth and be equally content in either circumstance because of the love and presence of Jesus.

If God has a deep longing to love the crown of his creation, he loves something that isn't a thing but a being of infinite value. The life that awakens to contentment discovered in God's glorious initiative is a life that pleases God. God doesn't long to love us because we somehow complete him or add to his glory. His longing is simply another demonstration of his grace. He longs to love because loving him in return is the zenith of the human experience. His longing is him taking the lead to show us our best life. The greatest life anyone could ever live is contentment, knowing and experiencing what it is to be forever loved by the Father.

I once met a man that predicted his death. When I met him, he was writing about how he wanted to die in a book titled *The Journey Home*. When the book was published, Dr. Bill Bright would already be in the presence of Jesus and never see the final edits. It didn't matter to him; he experienced it. When I met Dr. Bright, he was already nearing the end of his journey but was still gracious enough to give a twenty-three-year-old kid several hours one afternoon. I asked questions, listened intently to answers, and every once in a while, pinched myself to make sure I wasn't dreaming. I was sitting at the feet of the leader whom God had used, along with his equally incredible bride, Mrs. Vonette, to found Campus Crusade for Christ (now CRU). The organization had one mission in mind: to reach as many people with the good news of Jesus as possible. They had over twenty-five thousand staff and over half a million volunteers spread out over 190 countries, having a presence on almost every college and university campus in the world. Some have rightly acknowledged that Dr. Bright saw more people become followers of Jesus in his ministry than anyone in history, with the exception of the apostle Paul and maybe Dr. Billy Graham.

Yet, this is what he wrote about his death, just months before he passed from earth to glory:

> I want to die as if it were 1903, not 2003. . . .
> I do not want heroic and extraordinary mea-
> sures taken by the medical community as I
> leave this life. I am on my way to a better life,
> and I do not want to be waylaid or detoured

by the admirable but distracting technologies of the twenty-first century. I say "distracting" because compared to the glory of heaven and the physical presence of Jesus, they are nothing.[10]

It was Saturday, July 19, 2003, when Dr. Bright's breathing gradually began to slow. Mrs. Vonette recalled that late that evening, he was only taking four to four-and-a-half breaths per minute. She leaned down next to his ear and said, "I want you to go be with Jesus; you want to go be with Jesus, and Jesus wants you to come be with him. Why don't you let him carry you to heaven?" The next moment Bill Bright took his last breath on earth. His wife would later be comforted by the words of Saint Francis of Assissi: "For it is in dying, we are born to eternal life."[11]

When I think of Dr. Bright, though I only spent one afternoon in his presence, I think of someone who walked with Jesus. His contentment in life was evidence that he was loving Jesus. It was a contentment that matured and deepened with time. It could not be rushed or fully formed at a weekend retreat or conference. It's like the more he followed Jesus, the happier he was with Jesus, and the more he wanted to see Jesus. I want to live that way.

Contentment is not something you can touch or measure. The Puritans placed a significant emphasis on contentment and their writings that are still helpful today. Essentially, Puritans were a people in the late sixteenth and seventeenth centuries who wanted a purer church than the Church of England. Many of them came to the northern colonies of America, impacting and shaping much of New England. The

Puritan writers described contentment as a condition that was an art, a great mystery that could be learned. In *The Rare Jewel of Christian Contentment*, Jeremiah Burroughs defines it this way: "Christian contentment is that sweet, inward, quiet, gracious frame of spirit, which freely submits to and delights in God's wise and fatherly disposal in every condition."[12]

The apostle Paul once wrote: "I have learned to be content in whatever circumstances I find myself" (Phil. 4:11). Did you catch the first part?

"I have learned . . ."

Paul learned it, and so can we! He goes out of his way to emphasize the "I" in that statement. He had arrived at a place in his journey that only comes about by living a little while. He had journeyed to the condition of freely submitting and delighting in the good Father through thick and thin. On days when the sea breeze was a refreshing reminder of God's grace while pushing out of a port, and during nearly six years of incarceration in unimaginable and grotesque circumstances, his contentment deepened.

Paul's life echoes down through the ages that contentment isn't just about being satisfied with your situations or stuff; rather, it is all about being satisfied with Jesus in all of your circumstances. There is a joy to be found, a place to be discovered, and it can only be known once we have navigated some hurt and pain. Through which, whether it was a broken heart or a dark season, we experienced the sufficiency of a loving Father who was present.

That is not to say that contentment cannot be experienced to some degree early in our faith journey. Lately, I've been going through that crazy, out-of-body experience called teaching your firstborn kid to drive. Our lessons consist of teaching the basics over and over again. I find myself appreciating my own father's patience with my awkward attempts at guiding hundreds of horsepower of machinery. In a few short months, I've watched as he has grown more comfortable behind the wheel. His breathing is steadier, he doesn't have a death grip at ten-and-two, and he has learned that you don't have to put the weight of a small elephant on the brake to stop. In other words, he has become more confident while driving. Two reasons for this are happening simultaneously. For one, he has more experience driving. And for the other, he is trusting more in what he has learned about how to drive.

Paul teaches us that the more experience we have with God, the more comfortable we become with trusting God. In this sense, contentment is living and trusting more and more in what we are learning about being a child of God. It is learned by living, and the more we live, the more we learn. Remember, it is an art form that is mysterious. There is no paint-by-number plan for contentment. Just keep living and loving Jesus. And eventually, we'll wake up one day knowing that contentment is our traveling address as we journey through life and toward heaven, just like Dr. Bright.

Five Questions for Assessing Personal Contentment

Contentment is the key to much of what we have discussed in the last several chapters. When I am content, my relationships are healthier, my attitude is right, and my future moral vision is God-honoring. Then, I will have a reputation for honoring others, and my integrity will shine like stars in the world. How many marriages have been ruined, ethical lines crossed, churches damaged, pits of addiction fallen into—and the list could just go on—because of discontentment? The people with the least amount of happiness in this world live disappointed by the void of a misguided want for more. So often, we give an intense amount of energy for all the wrong things, then wonder why a star-filled night doesn't instill a sense of wonder. We should enjoy the moments in telling a story with our own lives. God hasn't called us to live vicariously through someone else. We were created to tell a story brimming with the theme of redemption. But when we are always the audience, we are never the artist. Our lives are a canvas that should be painted with brilliant colors of trust-filled living mesmerized by the amazement of grace.

While contentment can't be measured, it can be assessed. Therefore, let's ask ourselves several questions that help us evaluate whether we are learning to be content.

1. What am I loving? Do I give affection to the temporal while giving little attention to what matters for eternity? Do I long to know and see Jesus?

2. Is my ambition aimed at accumulation to enlarge my money, influence, material possessions, etc.? Or is my motivation in earning money, influence, and material possessions that I may steward them according to what pleases God?

3. Do my present dreams and aspirations in life align with the desires of God?

4. Am I at peace in my present circumstances? Am I experiencing the sufficiency of Jesus, a

peace that can only be given to a child of God, on the good and bad days?

5. Do I have the type of relationships in my life that nourish my soul and edify my life? Do I have friends who are delighting in God's wise and fatherly disposition during all seasons? Do I have a community that contributes to contentment in Jesus?

Stewarding Expectations

I love to have fun with my kids, and am a firm believer that our children need a mind full of memories that will remind them they are always loved unconditionally, cared for completely, and enjoyed consistently. So, we focus strategically on memories. We make up stories at the dinner table, go on quests to discover hidden treasure on our property (hidden because mythical creatures buried it there, of course!), have dance parties in our pajamas, and watch movies while eating mounds of popcorn. We also circle up together and study the Bible as a family and pray for each other. It's been long believed that our kids need our prayers. But the longer I live, the more I am convinced that I need theirs just as much. Christina and I hope our theory of parenting is right because we are over here laughing, crying, listening, talking, and just trying to love Jesus every day.

For the first ten years or so of our marriage, we had a television that was borderline antique. For you kids out there who haven't seen one, it was in the shape of a box, complete with "power," "channel," and "volume" buttons on the front. Several years ago, we decided it was time to trade it in for something newer. And by "we decided," I mean the television died and went to TV heaven. Thus began our entrance into "the age of flatscreens"! As we were shopping and trying to decide what to purchase next, my wife had an incredible idea. Now, in a chapter on contentment, you may be thinking we decided we were perfectly happy without a television, which would give us more time for talking and praying and reading the Bible. But you would be wrong.

Christina suggested that, since our family enjoyed watching movies together, and since my son and I kind of think college football is the greatest thing ever, let's get a really big one. I think I fell in love with her all over again at that moment. Believe it or not, there was a lot of wisdom in that suggestion. Think about it, there are eight of us; six kids, with my youngest being five and my oldest fifteen, and two adults (if you count me as an adult). And every week, we cuddle up in the den, usually on the weekend, and watch a movie or show. *It is so much fun!* I think it pleases our Father to see us bundled up in our pj's, enjoying a good story acted out on a flat electronic square. Our family time in the den is something all my kids anticipate. It often provides one-liners that will be repeated and are always a good illustration when we study the Bible. (All stories can only make sense in light of God's story.) It may be a temporary electronic thing, but we use it to have fun together and make memories that will hopefully outlast the flat electronic square.

You see, just because something is temporal doesn't mean that it is evil. Temporary things are blessings that can help or encourage us in the journey. And yes, that means that temporary things can bless us by allowing us to have fun with people we love or just give us rest. I guess the best way is for us to discern what temporary things can be gifts from God. It isn't wrong to desire temporary things, maybe like a nice television. The balancing act is to desire the right things without desire becoming the thing. In other words, we must steward our expectations so that they do not distract us from a life of contentment.

Whether it is in our education, careers, family, or social lives, stewarding our expectations cannot be understated. If contentment is an art form, and our lives a canvas, then our desires and expectations motivate the brush to be dipped into the various colors on the palette. As the masterpiece is slowly painted, the picture of contentment is often found in the presence of community, the service of others, and the love of a neighbor.

A person can be more content giving their only meal of the day to another in need rather than having enough money to feed an entire country. On the other hand, a person can be content earning lots of money and using it to help others, while the individual who has less money grows more cynical by the day. I do believe that it is harder to be rich and content than almost anything else. But in either case, a simple idea remains consistently resolute: *what we love will either destroy us or deliver us.*

If we care deeply about the things in the world that matter to God, then contentment is ours to enjoy no matter the season or circumstance of life. On the other hand, if we love money, status, power, brand, and pretty much anything else that doesn't please God, then discontentment is the strange bedfellow with us all our days. After all, "the kingdom of God is not eating and drinking, but righteousness, peace, and joy in the Holy Spirit" (Rom. 14:17). We either discover the treasure that is contentment, or it stays a mirage off in the distance and will never be known by what we love.

Let's finish our discussion on contentment with a question from Jesus: "What does it benefit someone to gain the whole world and yet lose his life?" (Mark 8:36). Many translations use the word *soul* instead of *life*. While that isn't necessarily bad, the Greek word that Jesus used is the same word translated "life" two times in the sentence before Jesus asks this question. While arguments could be made for either, there is a reason for mentioning the nuance. Jesus was talking about his philosophy of life and living. He was not teaching "what we must do to be saved from our sins." Only the blood of Jesus can accomplish that.[13] Jesus isn't teaching us how to be saved, but how to *live* saved. His philosophy was simply that the essence of our humanity is found in daily giving our life away. Self-interests have never led anyone to contentment. But serving the interests of God, that is really living.

The more we delight in the desires of God, the more peace we experience in this topsy-turvy world. The deeper our contentment, the less bound we are to the things of this world. And with contentment, the need to live someone else's dream seems to evaporate like water in a puddle on a scorching-hot day. When our home is in Jesus . . .

> it's okay if our stuff doesn't shine
>
> it's okay if we don't join the mad dash for more and more
>
> it's okay if we don't keep up, measure up, or stand out

it's okay if we don't drive the latest-model car
or live in the big house

It is okay because we are busy watching God paint a masterpiece on the canvas that is our lives. We aren't bored in Babylon or busy furnishing our lives with stuff that will never satisfy us. We decidedly are going to make good and wise decisions in a messed-up world and trust the song of grace that God wishes to sing over us. We're okay with "whatever will be, will be" because we trust in God's sovereignty. We are stewarding our expectations to align with God's desires and expectations. We are artists daily discovering the mystery that is contentment, busy submitting to and delighting in the desires of the good Father.

Conclusion

Echoes of the Ancient

Throughout the previous chapters, we have explored ten steps that must be taken if we are to experience the life God wants for us. Each step was built upon the life and teachings of Jesus and supported by a wide variety of Bible contributors. But Jesus wasn't just creating something new with his teaching concerning our ten steps; instead, he was fulfilling something old and true.

Long ago, and for the Jews *not* that far away, God made a promise. It began in the garden of Eden when Adam and Eve rebelled against the Lord's wishes. This promise set sail on a boat with two of every kind of animal and one family. It continued with an older couple too late in life to have children. The promise survived the worst kind of family dysfunction, forgetfulness, suffering, arrogance, and even nearly two million of God's people enslaved. We can understand the promise this way: the story will not end with rebellion or enslavement, but with redemption and eventual restoration, a life of freedom and joy with each sunrise for those who love Jesus.

Over and over again, God delivered a disobedient people all in accordance with his promise. You see, even if we forget or don't follow through on ours, God will always keep his promises. Way back in the Old Testament, to help his people live their best life, God gave his servant Moses ten commandments. These commandments were designed to help the people relate well to God and each other. In other words, you couldn't live your best life and ignore the instructions for your best life. But the commandments were not the fulfillment of God's promise; that mission was reserved for Jesus, which was actually and always God's plan, even before he created the world.

I purposely didn't mention that this was a book about the Ten Commandments out of a desire to demonstrate the timeless relevance of the ideas given to Moses thousands of years ago. It is incredible to think that God wanted what was best for his people then, as he still does today. And what has always been best is the fulfillment of a promise made way back in the garden: the coming of the Messiah. Jesus explicitly tells us that he came to complete all we had been taught about our best life:

> "Don't think that I came to abolish the Law or the Prophets. I did not come to abolish but to fulfill. For truly I tell you, until heaven and earth pass away, not the smallest letter or one stroke of a letter will pass away from the law until all things are accomplished. Therefore, whoever breaks one of the least of these commands and teaches others to do the same will be called least in the kingdom of heaven. But whoever does and teaches these commands will be called great in the kingdom of heaven." (Matt. 5:17–19)

In our day and age, we think the word *great* means something different than what was communicated in Jesus' statement. The idea of being called "great" versus "least" has to do with our approach to the teachings of Jesus as it pertains to the Ten Commandments. If we honor and treasure these teachings, then we live in the blessing of honor. On the other hand, if we trivialize Jesus' teaching about how to relate to God and others, then we really don't understand what an amazing gift grace has given us. It is akin to being given a nice house to live in, only to not take care of it. Within time, the paint is peeling, the roof is leaking, there are holes in the carpet, and the wood is rotting. We received a gift and treated it like junk. Maybe it's better said this way: we choose whether we are "least" or "great" in the kingdom of heaven by how we embrace and live a virtuous life.

Ten Steps Simplified into Two Steps ... that's Actually One Step

So now, it makes sense that we cannot even "speak about the Ten Commandments without relating them to the work of Jesus Christ." As followers of Jesus, we have been given a broader and deeper understanding than was ever possible at the foot of Mount Sinai.[1] As the Gospel writer John explained: "the law was given through Moses; grace and truth came through Jesus Christ" (John 1:17).

Jesus exemplifies wisdom that permeates through the stories of those who have lived a life built around the ten ideas that consumed these pages. It is almost as if there was something inherited or passed down from generation to generation. A person or generation of Christians can stand on the collective experience and wisdom from the narratives that made their story possible. What we now know is there was something that codifies, that binds together, those who lived well. If the collections of all the best lives lived were planets in a solar system, what sun are they orbiting around? Is there some bright light that illuminates all of those who, throughout the centuries, would dance across the stage of history? If such a discovery were made, would that not change everything by simplifying all that we have been taught? This was my aim in writing to you.

One last question . . .

What if it wasn't a discovery but, rather, a recovery of a simple, sacred strategy available for all?

It was C. S. Lewis who said, "People need to be reminded more often than they need to be instructed."[2] My hope has been to simply remind us of ideas that may have gotten lost in the debris left behind by the hurricanes of the pandemic. Or maybe these are instructions that were lost somewhere along the way between "What the heck is happening?" and "How in the world will I ever recover?" I am also optimistic that a longing will be stirred within each of us in being reminded of these truths, and not a longing for what once was, but a longing for what could be. You see, when we rediscover the life God has promised to us, our imaginations begin to fly beyond the stars with hope and possibility.

One last idea . . .

Love is the only way we can accomplish living our best lives.

Jesus taught,

> "Love the Lord your God with all your heart,
> with all your soul, and with all your mind.

This is the greatest and most important command. The second is like it: Love your neighbor as yourself. All the Law and the Prophets depend on these two commands." (Matt. 22: 37–40)

The love of Jesus is all we need to understand and experience our best life. It is the glue that holds everything together and the means by which we can accomplish every step discussed in the previous chapters.

There is no substitute for authentic love for Jesus. The love that God wants from us can't be faked. We have not entered into a contract with God that demands we give money, volunteer, go on mission trips, and whatever else is stipulated. The grace of Jesus cannot be reduced to a quid pro quo. No, we have entered into a covenant. We have responded to the grace of Jesus, who said, "Hey kid, come and follow me." Never forget this: you were chosen to be separated by the gospel of God. A covenant is all about promises being lived out in and through a relationship. It is a sacred agreement. In other words, we are all in on Jesus, and Jesus is all in on us. We are to love him with all of ourselves.

Now, let me say this next part a bit bluntly. We cannot love Jesus without also loving others. Jesus gave us one commandment, that at first seems like two, but is actually one. It is one commandment because of the undeniable correlation between loving God and loving everyone else. And I do think Jesus means *everyone*. He uses the word "neighbor," which is a simple way of saying, whoever is in your proximity. Let's be clear: Jesus wasn't talking about just loving fellow sisters and brothers in the Lord. Proximity means those around you as you navigate life's journey—the nice people, the weird people, the overly-confident-in-their-political-candidate people, the mean people, the redeemed people, and those in need of redemption. Paul would later emphasize this part of Jesus' teaching:

> The commandments, "Do not commit adultery; do not murder; do not steal; do not covet;" and any other commandment, are summed up by this commandment: "Love your neighbor as yourself." Love does no wrong to a neighbor. Love, therefore, is the fulfillment of the law. (Rom. 13:9–10)

Love is the only way to live. I mean, *really* live. Everything about the Ten Commandments is livable, and everything about Jesus' teaching on the subject is possible. Why? Because God's love made it possible. I am not suggesting, nor have I ever suggested, perfectionism. (The mention of the word is like nails on a chalkboard in my brain.) I am, however, suggesting that if we begin with God's love for us, and allow that love to motivate how we interact with others, then we can . . .

> Create a rhythm of renewal and live in the beginning place of God's goodness and grace

> Give up on the gods who aren't and spend our days chasing the light

> Fill the storeroom of our lives to overflow with goodness through the words we speak

> Enjoy rest in the journey so that we may journey well

Pursue healthy relationships built on love and honor

Calibrate the mentality of our hearts to have a Jesus tone to our daily living

Know every day we are more valuable to God than a galaxy

Be known as one who honors individual humans and all of human life

Shine like stars in the world through our character and trustworthiness

Submit and delight in the desires of the good Father

It is all possible because God is the keeper of all his promises. His love not only invites us into a life filled with his presence, but also shows us how to live there.

When We Love: Sunlight and Stars

We love because we belong to God, and showing his love is simply more opportunity to experience belonging. Think about that for a moment—we belong to Jesus. We live and love, belonging to Jesus. I wonder if we have lost the sense of what a big deal it is to belong to Jesus. Our rebellion and rejection of God's loving guidance de-created us to a point where we could only love "because he first loved us" (1 John 4:19). And still, to all our amazement and astonishment, Jesus made it possible for us to belong to the good Father again.

One cold night in Denver, Colorado, some friends asked if I had ever read any of Brennan Manning's works. Though I had heard of him and was faintly acquainted with his best-selling *Ragamuffin Gospel*, for whatever reason, I had never really explored his writings. Brennan was a different breed of believer altogether. He was a mystic, a Franciscan priest, and a recovering alcoholic. He lived in a cave for six months, served the most poverty-stricken people in society, and the list goes on. *Fascinating* and *intriguing* only begin to describe him. Anyway, I drove through the snow to a little community church on the outskirts of Denver, where we found our way into a half-full auditorium to hear him speak.

As he began to share that night, I was immediately captivated. I had never really heard anyone talk about God the way he did. There was such an emphasis on seeing God as our Father and we as his children. Though he went to heaven in 2013, I am still working my way through his books and sermons, and I am still captivated. In his book *The Furious Longing of God*, he explains the most powerful prayer that a child of God could pray:

"Abba, I belong to You."

He writes: "It's a prayer of exactly seven syllables, the number that corresponds perfectly to the rhythm of our breathing. As you inhale—*Abba*. As you exhale—*I belong to You*."[3] I want to challenge each of us to find a place where we can be alone and take ten uninterrupted minutes each day for one month, and there pray, "Abba, I belong to You" over and over. As you pray, imagine yourself to be a child crawling up into the familiar and trusting place that is your dad's lap. Begin to see God differently. Not as a taskmaster or your ticket to heaven, but as a Father who loves, likes, and wants to spend time with his child. I will make you this promise—it may be the most powerful experience of your life. With all that in mind, consider this: because you are Abba's child, you can live like you are being loved. You can live like you belong.

A friend of the eighteenth-century philosopher Edmund Burke said, following his death: "His virtues were his arts." I like to think Burke's friend described a life of strong beliefs that did not come across as dogmatic or stoic in any way. But rather, his beliefs were exemplified through his living in a harmonious and even artful manner.

I have tried to offer you ten steps to your best life. While each step builds on the last, they also cannot be understood in a completely linear fashion. And therein lies the art of it all. You have been created to create, to fill the canvas that is your life with radiant colors that all paint a picture of grace. Our brokenness has been made beautiful by the glorious gospel of God. Now, we get to tell a story where our virtues are our arts. In this book, I have only tried to give you the ingredients and point you in the right direction.

So, every day let the sun touch your skin and the stars capture your imagination. If you begin every day with gratitude and finish with wonder, then you will never waste a day. And wherever we may find ourselves, in whatever circumstance, "let us love one another, because love is from God" (1 John 4:7).

Notes

Introduction: Blue Tarps

1. Mark É. Czeisler, et al., "Mental Health, Substance Use, and Suicidal Ideation During the COVID-19 Pandemic—United States, June 24–30, 2020," CDC, August 14, 2020, https://www.cdc.gov/mmwr/volumes/69/wr/mm6932a1.htm?s_cid=mm6932a1_w.

2. Even as I write, the pandemic is an ever-evolving situation. Who knows where things will stand by the time you're reading this.

3. Alistair Begg, *The Spurgeon Study Bible* (Nashville: Holman Bible Publishers, 2017), 773.

4. Leonard Sweet, *The Three Hardest Words* (Colorado Springs: Waterbrook Press, 2006), 31.

Chapter 1: God

1. Sally Lloyd-Jones, *The Jesus Storybook Bible: Every Story Whispers His Name* (Grand Rapids: Zondervan, 2007), 35–36.

2. Edwin A. Blum, ed., *CSB Study Bible: Christian Standard Bible* (Nashville: Holman Bible Publishers, 2017), 1505.

3. R. C. H. Lenski, *Commentary on the New Testament: Matthew*, vol. 1 (Peabody, MA: Hendrickson Publishers, 2001), 285.

4. Albert M. Wells Jr., *Inspiring Quotations* (Nashville: Thomas Nelson Publishers, 1988), 78–79.

5. J. Douma, *The Ten Commandments: Manual for the Christian Life* (Phillipsburg, NJ: P&R Publishing Co., 1996), 28.

Chapter 2: Image

1. J. Douma, *The Ten Commandments: Manual for the Christian Life* (Phillipsburg, NJ: P&R Publishing Co., 1996), 36.

2. William Barclay, *The Ten Commandments for Today* (San Francisco: Harper & Row Publishers, 1983), 21.

3. Joy Davidman, *Smoke on the Mountain* (Philadelphia: Westminster Press, 1954), 39.

4. George Campbell Morgan, *The Ten Commandments* (Grand Rapids: Baker Book House, 1974), 28.

5. Lehman Strauss, *The Eleven Commandments* (Fincastle, VA: Scripture Truth Book Company, 1979), 46.

6. This statement was based on a number of scholarly works including Johannes P. Louw and Eugene A. Nida, *Greek-English Lexicon of the New Testament: Based on Semantic Domains*, electronic ed. of the 2nd edition, vol. 1 (New York: United Bible Societies, 1996), 539.

7. These words were written by the author.

Chapter 3: Words

1. https://www.bostonglobe.com/news/nation/2017/01/10/timeline-shooting-emanuel-ame-church-charleston/5ty2K0cAT2kcdrLWMjts8O/story.html (accessed November 18, 2020)

2. Mark Berman, "'I forgive you.' Relatives of Charleston church shooting victims address Dylann Roof," *Washington Post*, June 19, 2015, https://www.washingtonpost.com/news/post-nation/wp/2015/06/19/i-forgive-you-relatives-of-charleston-church-victims-address-dylann-roof/ (accessed November 18, 2020).

3. Jordyn Phelps, "The Story Behind President Obama Singing 'Amazing Grace' at Charleston Funeral," ABC News, July 7, 2015, https://abcnews.go.com/Politics/story-president-obama-singing-amazing-grace-charleston-funeral/story?id=32264346 (accessed November 18, 2020).

4. Robert Jamieson, A. R. Fausset, and David Brown, *Commentary Critical and Explanatory on the Whole Bible*, vol. 2 (Oak Harbor, WA: Logos Research Systems, Inc., 1997), 127.

5. Joseph M. Stowell, *The Weight of Your Words* (Chicago: Moody Press, 1998) was particularly helpful when writing this section of the chapter.

6. Augustine of Hippo, Sermons on Selected Lessons of the New Testament, in *Saint Augustin: Sermon on the Mount, Harmony of the Gospels, Homilies on the Gospels*, ed. Philip Schaff, trans. R. G. MacMullen, vol. 6 (New York: Christian Literature Company, 1888), 332–33.

7. Walter A. Elwell and Philip W. Comfort, *Tyndale Bible Dictionary* (Wheaton, IL: Tyndale House Publishers, 2001), 579.

8. https://www.dictionary.com/e/pop-culture/cancel-culture/#:~:text=Cancel%20culture%20refers%20to%20the,the %20form%20of%20group%20shaming (accessed November 20, 2020)

9. https://twitter.com/KB_HGA, posted on June 16, 2020

Chapter 4: Rest

1. https://www.nhlbi.nih.gov/health-topics/sleep-depriva-tion-and-deficiency#:~:text=Sleep%20plays%20an%20impor-tant%20role,pressure%2C%20diabetes%2C%20and%20stroke (accessed November 23, 2020)

2. "Only humans willingly delay sleep," Energydots, March 10, 2021, https://energydots.com/2021/03/only-humans-will-ingly-delay-sleep/.

3. Craig Blomberg, New American Commentary: *Matthew*, vol. 22 (Nashville: Broadman & Holman Publishers, 1992), 194.

4. William Barclay, ed., *The Gospel of Matthew*, vol. 2 (Philadelphia: Westminster John Knox Press), 1976.

5. Henry G. Liddell, *A Lexicon Abridged from Liddell and Scott's Greek-English Lexicon* (Oak Harbor, WA: Logos Research Systems, Inc., 1996), 59.

6. R. C. H. Lenski, *Commentary on the New Testament: Mark*, vol. 4 (Peabody, MA: Hendrickson Publisher, 2001), 260.

7. Summarized from Gleason L. Archer, *A Survey of the Old Testament Introduction* (Chicago: Moody Press, 1974), 242–43.

8. Carl F. Keil and Franz Delitzsch, *Commentary on the Old Testament*, vol. 1 (Peabody, MA: Hendrickson, 1996), 417.

9. John Chrysostom, Homilies of St. John Chrysostom, Archbishop of Constantinople, on the Epistle to the Hebrews in *Saint Chrysostom: Homilies on the Gospel of St. John and Epistle to the Hebrews*, ed. Philip Schaff, trans. Thomas Keble and Frederic Gardiner, vol. 14 (New York: Christian Literature Company, 1889), 455.

10. Brent Crowe, *Moments 'til Midnight* (Nashville: B&H Publishing Group, 2018), 220.

11. Colin Bertram, "Eric Clapton: The Unthinkable Tragedy That Inspired 'Tears in Heaven,'" Biography, May 6, 2020, https://www.biography.com/news/eric-clapton-tears-in-heaven-son (accessed November 25, 2020).

12. "Tears in Heaven" written by Eric Patrick Clapton and Will Jennings, lyrics © Universal Music Publishing Group, Warner Chappell Music, Inc.

Chapter 5: Relationships

1. Carl F. Keil and Franz Delitzsch, *Commentary on the Old Testament*, vol. 1. (Peabody, MA: Hendrickson, 1996), 400.

2. Brent Crowe, *Reimagine: What the World Would Look Like If God Got His Way* (Colorado Springs: NavPress, 2013.

3. Leon Morris, *Testaments of Love: A Study of Love in the Bible* (Grand Rapids: Eerdmans Publishing Company, 1981), 116.

4. Brent Crowe, *Moments 'til Midnight* (Nashville: B&H Publishing Group, 2018), 55–62.

5. C. S. Lewis, *The Four Loves* (New York: Harcourt, Inc., 1988), 63.

6. Morris, *Testaments of Love: A Study of Love in the Bible*, 120–21.

7. Taken from the song "Holy" written by Tone Jones, Michael Pollack, Jorgen Odegard, Justin Bieber, Chance the

Rapper, Jon Bellion, TBHits & Mr. Franks, released September 18, 2020.

8. Summarized from Eric Metaxas, *Bonhoeffer: Pastor, Martyr, Prophet, Spy* (Nashville: Thomas Nelson, 2010).

9. These five points are taken from Dietrich Bonhoeffer, *Sanctorum Communio: A Theological Study of the Sociology of the Church*, ed. Clifford J. Green and Joachim von Soosten, trans. Richard Krauss and Nancy Lukens, vol. 1 (Minneapolis: Fortress Press, 2009), 168–70.

Chapter 6: Attitude

1. Larry L. Rasmussen, ed., "Editor's Introduction to the English Edition," in Dietrich Bonhoeffer, Dietrich Bonhoeffer Works: Berlin: 1932–1933, eds. Carsten Nicolaisen and Ernst-Albert Scharffenorth, trans. Isabel Best, David Higgins, and Douglas W. Stott, vol. 12 (Minneapolis, MN: Fortress Press, 2009), 3.

2. Barbara Winton, *If It's Not Impossible: The Life of Sir Nicholas Winton* (Padstow, Cornwall: Troudbador Publishing Ltd., 2014), 24.

3. To know more about Sir Nicholas Winton, I strongly encourage you to read *If It's Not Impossible* by Barbara Winton, daughter of Nicholas and Grete Winton.

4. William E. Vine, *An Expository Dictionary of New Testament Words* (Old Tappan, NJ: Frank Revell Company, 1966), 147.

5. Kenneth S. Wuest, *Wuest's Word Studies from the Greek New Testament: For the English Reader*, vol. 8 (Grand Rapids: Eerdmans, 1997), 118.

6. Merrill C. Tenney, ed., *The Zondervan Pictorial Encyclopedia of the Bible,* vol. 4 (Grand Rapids: Zondervan Publishing, 1975), 747–48.

Chapter 7: Worthiness

1. Tim Keller, "5 Features That Made the Early Church Unique," January 10, 2020, https://www.thegospelcoalition.org /article/5-features-early-church-unique/ (accessed December 1, 2020).

2. Ibid.

3. Dietrich Bonhoeffer, *Creation and Fall: A Theological Exposition of Genesis 1–3*, eds. Martin Rüter, Ilse Tödt, and John W. de Gruchy, trans. Douglas S. Bax, vol. 3 (Minneapolis: Fortress Press, 2004), 99.

4. Ibid.

5. Poem written by the author.

6. Andrew Sullivan, *Virtually Normal* (New York: Vintage Publishing, 1996), opening statements.

7. William Lane Craig, *Hard Questions, Real Answers* (Wheaton, IL: Crossway Books, 2003), 133–34.

8. J. S. Feinberg, P. D. Feinberg, and A. Huxley, *Ethics for a Brave New World* (Wheaton, IL: Crossway Books, 1996, c1993).

9. John Calvin, *Golden Booklet of the True Christian Life* (Grand Rapids: Baker Book House, 1977), 57.

Chapter 8: Respect

1. Kathleen M. Chambers, *Oswald Chambers: The Best from All His Books* (Nashville: Thomas Nelson, 1987), 289.

2. https://www.sparknotes.com/nofear/shakespeare/julius-caesar/page_234/ (accessed November 27, 2020)

3. Merriam-Webster, I. *Merriam-Webster's Collegiate Dictionary* 10th ed. (Springfield, MA: Merriam-Webster, 1996).

4. Carl F. Keil and Franz Delitzsch, *Commentary on the Old Testament,* vol. 1 (Peabody, MA: Hendrickson, 1996), 400.

5. David R. Schaffer, *Social and Personality Development* (Florence: Wadsworth Publishing 2008), 64.

6. William Barclay, ed., *The Letters of James and Peter* (Philadelphia: Westminster John Knox Press, 1976).

7. Edwin A. Blum, ed., *CSB Study Bible: Christian Standard Bible* (Nashville: Holman Bible Publishers, 2017), 1963.

8. Victor Hugo, *Les Misérables* (London, England: Penguin Books, 1987), 521.

9. Blum, *CSB Study Bible: Christian Standard Bible*, 1540.

10. Kenneth S. Wuest, *Wuest's Word Studies from the Greek New Testament: For the English Reader*, vol. 1 (Grand Rapids: Eerdmans, 1997), 233–34.

11. John Chrysostom, Homilies of St. John Chrysostom, Archbishop of Constantinople, on the Epistle to the Hebrews in *Saint Chrysostom: Homilies on the Gospel of St. John and Epistle to the Hebrews*, ed. Philip Schaff, trans. Thomas Keble and Frederic Gardiner, vol. 14 (New York: Christian Literature Company, 1889), 427.

12. William Barclay, ed., *The Gospel of Luke* (Philadelphia: Westminster John Knox Press, 1975).

Chapter 9: Integrity

1. https://www.pewresearch.org/fact-tank/2019/07/22/key-findings-about-americans-declining-trust-in-government-and-each-other/ (accessed December 6, 2020)

2. J. A. Motyer, *The Message of Philippians* (Downers Grove, IL: InterVarsity Press, 1984), 133.

3. https://catholictruth.net/CTNet_RC/en/archive.asp?d=20150820 (accessed December 6, 2020)

4. https://books.google.com/books?id=f2lKAAAAYAAJ&pg=PA800&lpg=PA800&dq=St.+Bernard+%22I+have+freed+my+soul%22&source=bl&ots=6p_qjnAlHY&sig=ACfU3U0pvskbdlItBLemA3Neu5SIjt9h1A&hl=en&sa=X&ved=2ahUKEwjnjuiE35ftAhUSy1kKHdLLD2oQ6AEwEHoECAsQAg#v=onepage&q=St.%20Bernard%20%22I%20have%20freed%20my%20soul%22&f=falsen (accessed December 7, 2020)

Chapter 10: Contentment

1. Jerry Bridges, *Respectable Sin* (Colorado Springs: Navpress, 2007), 71.

2. J. I. Packer, *Knowing God* (Downers Grove, IL: InterVarsity Press, 1973), 31.

3. Avraham Negev, *The Archaeological Encyclopedia of the Holy Land*, 3rd ed. (New York: Prentice Hall Press, 1990).

4. Stephen R. Miller, New American Commentary: *Daniel,* vol. 18 (Nashville: Broadman & Holman Publishers, 1994), 59.

5. Walter A. Elwell and Philip W. Comfort, *Tyndale Bible Dictionary* (Wheaton, IL: Tyndale House Publishers, 2001), 855.

6. *The Greatest Showman Musical*, 2017.

7. Neil Postman, *Amusing Ourselves to Death* (New York: Penguin Books, 1985), 155–56.

8. Craig Blomberg, New American Commentary: *Matthew,* vol. 22 (Nashville: Broadman & Holman Publishers, 1992), 123.

9. Brennan Manning, *The Furious Longing of God* (Colorado Springs: David C. Cook, 2009), 24.

10. Bill Bright, *The Journey Home: Finishing with Joy* (Nashville: Thomas Nelson Publishers, 2003), 115.

11. Ibid., 171.

12. Jeremiah Burroughs, *The Rare Jewel of Christian Contentment* (Carlisle, PA: Banner of Truth Trust, 1979), 19.

13. Kenneth S. Wuest, *Wuest's Word Studies from the Greek New Testament: For the English Reader*, vol. 1. (Grand Rapids: Eerdmans, 1997), 171–72.

Conclusion: Echoes of the Ancient

1. The idea in this sentence and the quote from the previous sentence are credited to J. Douma, *The Ten Commandments* (Phillipsburg, NJ: P&R Publishing, 1996), 5.

2. C. S. Lewis, *Mere Christianity* (New York: HarperCollins, 2015), 82.

3. Brennan Manning, *The Furious Longing of God* (Colorado Springs: David C. Cook, 2009), 46.